Crisis Management
in
Japan *&*
the United States

Creating Opportunities for
Cooperation amid Dramatic Change

A Joint U.S.-Japan Research Project Conducted by
The Institute for Foreign Policy Analysis
The Osaka School for International Public Policy (Osaka University)

Edited by
James L. Schoff

A Publication by

The Institute for Foreign Policy Analysis, Inc.
In Association with The Fletcher School of Law
and Diplomacy, Tufts University

Brassey's Inc.

Brassey's, Inc.

(Editorial)   22841 Quicksilver Dr., Dulles, VA 20166 USA

(Orders)   Brassey's Book Orders, P.O. Box 960, Herndon, Virginia 22070 USA

Library of Congress Cataloging-in-Publication Data

Crisis Management in Japan and the United States

ISBN: 1-57488-894-3; $25.00

CIP information not ready at time of publication

Designed by J. Christian Hoffman

Printed in the United States of America by Merrill/Daniels Press, Everett, Massachusetts

10 9 8 7 6 5 4 3 2 1

Contents

⸭

Illustrations

✦

Foreword

✢

As this study documents, the last few years have been a period of gradual, but historically dramatic change in Japan's approach to crisis situations – natural or man-made – and the management of their consequences. Significant steps have been taken, especially since the September 11, 2001, attacks in the United States, to set in place the legal framework and organizational structure for a more responsive and effective Japanese crisis management system, and to clarify when and how Japan's Self-Defense Forces (SDF) – which maintain many response capabilities that could be vital to disaster relief and other emergency operations – may be allowed to contribute to a national or international crisis response team. So, too, given his central role in promoting these improvements, Prime Minister Junichiro Koizumi's re-election in September 2003 to another three-year term as president of the ruling Liberal Democratic Party (LDP), together with the LDP-led coalition's retention of governmental power (albeit by a slim margin) after the November 2003 elections for the Lower House of Japan's Diet, suggests that the stage is now set for still more efforts by Tokyo to strengthen Japan's capacity to take action in crisis situations, whether they occur within its national territory, in the areas surrounding Japan, or even farther afield (in Iraq, for instance).

That said, much more work still needs to be done. This is especially true with respect to what can and cannot be done in the more ambiguous realm of peacetime crisis management situations, where the precise origin and nature of an event demanding a response may be unclear, as well as the immediacy of the risk to Japan's own security (narrowly defined) and the appropriateness of using Japanese SDF units to respond, even in the carefully circumscribed manner that is currently allowed. For evidence on this score, one need only consider the cautious manner that Koizumi – confronted with a stronger Democratic Party of Japan (DPJ) opposition in the wake of the November Diet elections – was forced to adopt in pursuing the question of dispatching some one thousand SDF troops to Iraq in the closing weeks of 2003. Some degree of hesitancy, of course, can be traced to the fact that the dispatch to Iraq would be Japan's first overseas deployment of ground combat forces since World War II (and could, as a result, give rise to criticism by Japan's neighbors, who still worry over the prospect of Japanese militarism in the future), but a good deal of Tokyo's caution may be rooted as well in the need to weigh carefully (and respond wisely to) concerns expressed by the Japanese public over the potential consequences for Japan – such as a possible increase in terrorist attacks within Japanese territory – of committing the SDF to a relatively distant military theater that remains quite unstable. Even among those who favor a higher profile for Japan in the international security realm, there is worry that potential SDF casualties in Iraq on par, for example, with those suffered by the Italian or Spanish contingents could reverse in one fell swoop all their carefully orchestrated efforts to nudge Tokyo beyond its classic "homeland defense only" mentality.

It is true, to be sure, that much has been accomplished in the area of crisis management planning over the last several years to help ease Japan's traditional reluctance to consider military deployments in crisis response situations. Critical in this regard was the adoption of the International Peace Cooperation Law (commonly referred to as the peacekeeping, or PKO, law) in 1992, the approval of the Revised Guidelines for U.S.-Japan Defense Cooperation in 1997, the passage of special anti-terrorism legislation in November 2001 (leading to the consistent provision of Maritime SDF logistical support to operation Enduring Freedom, or OEF, since that time), the dispatch of an *Aegis* destroyer to the Indian Ocean in December 2002 as part of the OEF support, the approval of a special package of national emergency legislation by the Diet in June 2003, and the subsequent Diet vote in July 2003 to approve, in principle, the sending of SDF units to Iraq. But as helpful as these various initiatives have been for those advocating a more forward-leaning posture for Japan with regard to regional and global security challenges, they have not – as the debate over the dispatch of troops to Iraq served again to illustrate – removed all uncertainty with respect to when and under what authority Tokyo may respond to crises beyond the Japanese home islands, and, when it does choose to do so, with what level and mix of civilian and military assets. So, while public debate on such matters may become more open and pointed in the years ahead, there will likely be no easy or predictable answers, except perhaps in situations where there is a direct armed attack (or credible threat thereof) against Japan proper.

It is with an eye to future debate, moreover, that the potentially restraining influence of the November 2003 parliamentary election results – which furthered the transition to a two (major)-party political system in Japan – cannot be ignored or underestimated. The DJP increased its strength in the Lower House by roughly 40 percent since the last election, in 2000, and it has staked out a more restrictive position with regard to the deployment of Japan's SDF overseas, one that emphasizes peacekeeping (as opposed to peace enforcement) duties conducted in support of a clear United Nations mandate. Though it opposed the U.S.-led war in Iraq and any direct SDF role in support of that operation, the DPJ does agree that Japan now shares with the international community as a whole a responsibility to help reconstruct Iraq, but it should do that, DPJ leaders argue, solely with civilian teams. If SDF units are ever sent to Iraq (or similar locations), specific prior approval, the DPJ goes on to stress, ought to be secured from the Diet for each deployment. At the very least, then, gains made by the DPJ – as well as by the LDP's more pacifist-minded, Buddhist-influenced coalition partner, Komeito – are likely to increase the clout of those in Japan who want to help internationally, but in a strictly non-military manner. Looking ahead, such a turn of events may put a damper on LDP plans to draw on the dispatch of Japanese troops to Iraq – and on what Prime Minister Koizumi and his advisors hope will be a record of success for the SDF in that endeavor – to bring forward follow-on legislation in the first half of 2004 to the historic laws passed in June 2003 regarding allowable actions by the SDF during an armed attack on Japan or a major domestic emergency, perhaps broadening them to cover more effectively a wider range of non-attack and non-Japan-centered crisis scenarios.

Beyond considerations of party politics and legislative reform, there is also the more amorphous, but still vitally important, task of cultivating the necessary mindset in Japan for establishing a more responsive crisis management system to conduct operations within (and around) the home islands, as well as for undertaking international security operations, using in both cases the SDF more effectively. In many ways, successive cabinets in Japan have tackled the easiest problems first, adjusting legal mechanisms, tinkering with organization charts, and clarifying responsibility and accountability in a generic sense. Ushering in real change in Japanese attitudes on these and related issues, however, is an entirely different proposition, and it is a task that is far from complete. Indications are that not only has the voting public yet to make up its mind regarding the SDF's role in pending national security and crisis management reforms, but many politicians, bureaucrats, and even those within the SDF itself have not reached a full consensus on how best to proceed to meet these new challenges. It is one thing, moreover, to decide that SDF personnel should be sent to assist in troubled areas around the world, but still another matter altogether to properly recruit, equip, and train those forces for the new types of missions they will be required to perform. Sorting all of this out will not happen quickly, and only time will tell if the momentum generated over the past few years will outlast the current Koizumi administration. We suspect that it will, for as important as the prime minister and his supporters have been in the recent shift toward a more active Japanese security posture, the desire to move in this direction appears to be fairly widespread, and not limited to a single political party (or, for that matter, political leader). Still, this is a delicate time in Japan's emergence as a more confident player on the international security stage, and, as alluded to already, a catastrophe in Iraq involving Japanese soldiers once they are deployed could ultimately harm, rather than help, this process.

None of this means, of course, that bold and meaningful action on the part of Japan beyond that already taken will not happen. To the contrary, the decision taken by the Koizumi cabinet on December 9, 2003, to move forward with the troop dispatch to Iraq confirms a willingness to become more directly engaged in international security operations, even in risky environments. As for crisis situations within Japanese territory (or waters), the case studies outlined in this monograph, and the lessons learned to which they gave rise, provide more than enough evidence of Japan's capacity and intention to strengthen its response capabilities for such situations in both the civil and military sectors, whether the crisis at hand be the result of a natural disaster, a major industrial accident, or a deliberate act of violence. Indeed, despite Japan's past shortcomings in handling major crises, and despite its past aversion to greater reliance on the SDF in domestic or international emergencies, Japan is clearly becoming a more willing and competent partner for the United States in the broad realm of crisis and consequence management. The United States should embrace this change, and work closely with Japan to further cement better policy planning and organizational ties. The timing for such collaboration is particularly opportune, as both countries are still in the process of reforming vital institutions and policies to manage and guide crisis and consequence management operations, but they have yet to establish lasting habits or clear procedures for bilateral cooperation to the degree desired and needed. Over the last several years, the United States and Japan, individually and together, have accomplished much and set in place a solid base of cooperation upon which to build, but there is, as we noted at the outset, a lot of important work left to do. It is our hope that this study will help point the way toward more productive avenues for cooperation in the future, and will motivate both countries to move in those directions.

Charles M. Perry

Jacquelyn K. Davis

December 2003

Preface

✢

Over the past few decades, the United States and Japan have developed an ever thickening web of cooperative and consultative relationships across various fields including the arts, sciences, culture, economics, education, politics, and the military. Mirroring the trends of technological development, globalization, and greater interdependence among nations, an increasingly wide variety of institutions and working professionals from the two countries are collaborating on countless projects, some with commercial applications, others focused on alleviating poverty, disease, and environmental degradation in the developing world, and still others aimed at protecting national and international security. The primary motivating factor behind these efforts is the quality and often complementary nature of the countries' financial, technical, and human resources available to address such problems or exploit opportunities, as well as ever strengthening common interests with regard to nurturing global economic health, promoting democracy, and maintaining a stable international order. Despite significant language and cultural barriers, citizens of the world's top two economies continue to explore new ways to work together. A recent example of this trend is the increased cooperation between Japanese and U.S. non-governmental organizations and civil society organizations in the areas of advocacy and overseas development (a field that previously saw relatively little U.S.-Japan cooperation).

The same forces that bring Americans and Japanese together in pursuit of constructive objectives, however, also allow for greater and more rapid harm when a natural or man-made calamity occurs, and preparing to manage large-scale crises and their consequences is proving to be yet another necessary avenue for bilateral cooperation. Improvements in communications, computing, transportation, and other technologies; increased trade and more integrated economic activity; and a broad U.S.-Japan political and military alliance in global affairs have contributed to general prosperity, but they have also had negative effects that could potentially outstrip the ability of a single nation to respond adequately on its own. Examples of these negative effects include more sophisticated military threats (missiles and weapons of mass destruction in North Korea and other hostile states), quick-moving information technology threats (global computer viruses and threats to critical infrastructure), the fast spread of infectious diseases across borders (evidenced by the outbreak of severe acute respiratory syndrome, or SARS, in 2003), cascading economic failures (as seen in the Asian financial crisis in the late 1990s), and asymmetric threats that cut across all the above-mentioned examples (via non-state terrorism and the proliferation of chemical, biological, and nuclear materials, not to mention the spread of radical and violent ideologies underlying these threats, the adherents of which see themselves in competition with democracy and capitalism). In addition, the concentration of people and vital infrastructure in urban centers means that a large-scale natural disaster, such as a massive earthquake, could have a devastating human and economic impact in cities like Tokyo or Los Angeles. The two countries also have an opportunity and an obligation to assist third countries when they are faced with natural and man-made catastrophes. All of these facts argue for improved national and international crisis management efforts on the part of the United States and Japan, but particularly Japan, where a disaster could have a substantial impact not only on Japanese security, but also on U.S.

security because of the critical role that Japan plays as a host to U.S. military forces.

In light of this need, the Osaka School of International Public Policy (OSIPP) at Osaka University and the Institute for Foreign Policy Analysis (IFPA), under a generous grant from the United States-Japan Foundation, in 2000 began a multi-year project to examine ways to enhance U.S.-Japanese cooperation on crisis and consequence management. At the start of the project, the co-organizers believed that bilateral consultation in this field was inadequate and that Japan in particular needed to improve its crisis management system after its poor execution during such events as the Great Hanshin-Awaji Earthquake in 1995 and the Tokaimura nuclear plant accident in 1999. The primary goal of this undertaking, therefore, was to address these inadequacies by promoting greater cross-fertilization of people, ideas, and best practices in the general field of crisis management so that both countries would be better prepared in case of various national, regional, or global emergencies.

Over the course of this project, however, participants have noticed significant improvements in the areas of both bilateral cooperation and Japanese domestic reform. Consequently, this monograph has become as much an explanation of the dramatic changes that have recently taken place as it is a call to action for further enhancements. By researching and explaining these recent developments, the project aims to assist crisis management professionals and alliance managers in identifying the most efficient and productive means of cooperation. During the past three years, this project has played its part in promoting bilateral dialogue and in providing statistical and intellectual weight behind the consultations and reform, the very importance of which was underlined in a most tragic and unexpected way by the horrible terrorist attacks in the United States on September 11, 2001.

As part of the project, the two institutions organized and held two conferences – the first in Washington, D.C., in November 2000 and the second in Tokyo in April 2002 – that brought together government, academic, and private sector experts to examine the issues raised in crisis and consequence management situations and to review current and potential future national and international responses to disaster situations. This monograph is an outgrowth of discussions held at these two conferences, papers presented at the meetings, and substantial research since the second conference to take into account the dramatic changes taking place in both countries.

The monograph is divided into five chapters. The first introduces the context behind some of the major reforms involving crisis and consequence management in both the United States and Japan. This provides a basis for seeing how each government views its responsibilities and the scope of the problems at hand. It also provides insight into what organizations and capabilities are viewed as necessary to respond to various crises and disasters. Definitional, cultural, and legal clarity also helps highlight differences and similarities between the Japanese and U.S. approaches to the issues (contributing to constructive collaboration), and the second chapter provides this necessary input. The third chapter presents four case studies in crisis management – two in Japan, one in the United States, and one thematic case study on cyber security. The studies highlight both current and past mechanisms for crisis response and consequence management in each country, as well as the past organizations. They also provide insights into areas that may be amenable to future collaboration. The fourth chapter of the monograph builds on the first three and examines how the threat of both man-made and natural disasters has evolved, and how the mechanisms to detect and respond have similarly evolved in Japan and the United States. Various laws, procedures, and organizational changes are examined, and open questions and ongoing policy issues are highlighted. For the United States, changes both before and after September 11 are outlined, and the summer 2002 initiative to create an entirely new cabinet-level department with responsibilities in this area is discussed. The fifth and final section contains conclusions and recommendations, focusing on the most promising areas for cooperation and collaboration between the United States and Japan in crisis and consequence management.

IFPA and OSIPP are grateful to the United States-Japan Foundation for its support of this research and dialogue project. It has been a true bilateral effort in terms of organizational and intellectual contribution, and the project has facilitated substantive meetings among dozens of Japanese and American specialists who normally have few, if any, opportunities to interact and exchange ideas and information. In this sense, we believe that the project has taken to heart the Foundation's goal of building bridges between our two nations, and that the benefits of these cooperative efforts will be felt by many for a long time to come. Crisis management cooperation between the United States and Japan is beginning to thrive, and this project was fortunately timed to catch this cresting wave of interest.

Professor Toshiya Hoshino of OSIPP and Dr. Charles M. Perry of IFPA led the Japanese- and American-side teams for this project respectively. They would like to thank several people for their contributions to the project, including, in Japan, Professor Mitsuru Kurosawa of OSIPP, Professor Satoshi Morimoto of Takushoku University, Professor Toshiyuki Shikata of Teikyo University, and Professor Takashi Kawakami of Hokuriku University, as well as Mr. Hideshi Tokuchi, counselor in the Office of the Assistant Chief Cabinet Secretary for National Security Affairs and Crisis Management, among others. Also, Professor Tomohito Shinoda, of the International University of Japan, and Ms. Yumiko Nakagawa at OSIPP provided important research assistance at critical times. In the United States, the project directors would like to thank Dr. Andrew C. Winner, now at the U.S. Naval War College, who drafted a significant portion of this monograph in its early stages; James L. Schoff of IFPA for his work drafting and editing the final version of the book; Dr. Jacquelyn K. Davis of IFPA for her insight, advice, and contributions to the dialogues at the core of the project; as well as Derek Boc, Christian Hoffman, Jack Kelly, Adelaide Ketchum, and Toshi Yoshihara of IFPA for their valuable assistance. The organizers are also grateful to all of the talented men and women who contributed to the success of this project by participating in the two conferences. All of the conference participants are listed in the appendix at the end of the monograph, along with descriptions of the meetings.

CHAPTER ONE

Overview

Change & Opportunity

✦

In the aftermath of the September 11, 2001, terrorist attacks in the United States, crisis management is no longer a concept that is known primarily to esoteric defense and security communities in the United States and Japan. The ability of governments to respond to a range of crises – from natural disasters to catastrophes precipitated by malevolent actors – has become a subject of increasing importance to a far broader community in both countries. In fact, each has been working diligently over the last decade or so to improve its own crisis management capabilities, and the two allies have also been cooperating to enhance their ability to respond jointly when appropriate. The attacks on September 11 and the subsequent global war on terrorism (GWOT) merely accelerated a deliberate process that was already underway in the United States and Japan. In many ways, the speed with which both countries drastically reformed their organizational and legal structures related to crisis management has been astounding, including the establishment of a new cabinet-level department in the United States (the Department of Homeland Security); a series of new laws and administrative changes governing the activities of Japan's Self-Defense Forces (SDF), its Security Council (Anzen Hoshō Kaigi), and other offices involved in crisis management decision making; and the revamping of a special U.S.-Japan bilateral coordinating mechanism and planning process for certain emergencies in and surrounding Japan. Additional reforms are expected in the next few years. As just one example of the unprecedented level of attention these issues are attracting, Japan's prime minister has even proposed carrying out a national referendum on revising the country's constitution, in part on national security and crisis management grounds, which would be the first attempt to do so under Japan's post-World War II constitution.[1]

This research project began with the premise that the systems for crisis management and communication in both countries required improvement (particularly in the case of Japan), and that the two nations would benefit from greater cooperation in this field, as well as in the area of dealing with the consequences of a catastrophic nuclear, biological, or chemical (NBC) accident or attack. Both project collaborators – IFPA and OSIPP – believed that the United States needed to reach out more aggressively to share its expertise and assets with key allies in order to extend its perimeter of preparedness. At the same time, policy makers and security experts in Japan were anxious to enhance their country's crisis management capabilities and decision-making processes, and working with the United States on these issues was viewed as advantageous in this regard and as an opportunity to make better use of the U.S.-Japan alliance. The project was designed, therefore, to inform Japanese and U.S. government officials about the general crisis management experiences in both countries, assess trends and specific changes with regard to crisis and consequence management planning, and identify opportunities for improving bilateral cooperation and for the allies to take a leadership role in regional or global efforts. The project purposefully chose to consider a broad range of crisis types (natural, man-made, financial, medical, physical, cyber-based, etc.), rather than choose one or two types of potential disaster situations, so that the most promising avenues for cooperation might be identified. The project team generally agreed that it made sense for the United States and Japan to try to move crisis/consequence management functions into the mainstream of alliance activities, though this was believed to be a longer-term goal given the lack of an appropriate legal basis in Japan for dealing with certain large-scale domestic emergencies, let alone legislation governing the conduct of certain joint U.S.-Japan operations within or surrounding Japan. Events in the past few years significantly sped up the pace of reform, however, especially in Japan.

What the project team did not expect was that circumstances would change as dramatically as they did, and in many respects Japan has accomplished in the past three years what in less threatening times would likely have taken a decade or two (details of these changes are discussed in chapter 4). The impetus for change came not only from the September 11 terrorist attacks and the the GWOT, but also from North Korea's withdrawal from the Nuclear Non-Proliferation Treaty (NPT) and its overt pursuit of a ballistic missile arsenal armed with nuclear or chemical weapons, as well as the sinking of a North Korean spy/drug-running ship near Japan's Amami-Oshima Islands. The agents of change included a fortuitous mix of political leaders (such as Prime Minister Junichiro Koizumi, former Deputy Chief Cabinet Secretary Shinzo Abe, Defense Agency Director Shigeru Ishiba, Tokyo Governor Shintaro Ishihara, and others), who were willing to press the issues publicly and in the Diet (Japan's parliament) to enact various legal and organizational reforms and confront taboos regarding the deployment of Japan's SDF. Because reform has been reactionary and driven by events, however, the result is a patchwork of laws, offices, and budgets that require further review and augmentation before they are sufficient *and* efficient. Similarly, cooperation between the United States and Japan in this area has surged ahead in some cases (such as the SDF logistical support mission in the Indian Ocean for U.S. and allied military operations in Afghanistan), but is lagging in others (as in the slow progress in fine tuning the bilateral coordination mechanism for use in certain emergency situations in Japan). The organizers of this project are overall heartened by the significant progress made in the past few years in terms of strengthening Japan's crisis management system and the process of bilateral cooperation, but at the same time they notice gaps that should be addressed and opportunities that can be exploited (perhaps even created) in the future.

Establishing effective methods and modes of bilateral cooperation in the area of crisis and consequence management is a moving target because of the legal and organizational changes underway not only in Japan, but also in the United States. In many respects the United States, with its streamlined decision-making structure, highly professionalized Federal Emergency Management Agency (FEMA), and the unique ability of state governors to call up National Guard forces, was seen as a potential model for Japan to follow in terms of revising its own crisis management system. Now the proposed model itself is changing, demonstrated in part by the creation of the Department of Homeland Security and other reforms in the United States. In addition, the U.S. military is also looking to realign its force structure globally, which could have implications for the availability of certain assets and methods of cooperation with other countries' armed forces. The project organizers see these changes as an opportunity to create more consistent and efficient methods of crisis and consequence management cooperation between the United States and Japan. To make the most of this opportunity, however, it is important for both parties to understand the context of crisis management evolution in each country, as well as the current status of domestic reform and bilateral cooperative efforts and structures.

The Rising Profile of Crisis Management

In Japan, the topic of improving its crisis management capabilities was already on a slow burn in the 1990s. During that decade, Japan confronted a series of large-scale national disasters and crises – some natural and some man-made – that sorely tested the response capabilities of the government and highlighted its shortcomings. The 1995 Great Hanshin-Awaji Earthquake, the sarin gas attack by the Aum Shinrikyo cult on the Tokyo subway system that same year, the Tokaimura nuclear accident in 1999, and the North Korean launch of a *Taepodong* missile over the land and airspace of Japan in 1998 (together with regular infiltration by North Korean spy boats of Japanese coastal waters), among other cases, each highlighted different problems that the Japanese government faced in dealing with these complex contingencies. The public reaction to the incidents and the responses by the Japanese government led to various efforts on the part of authorities to improve response procedures and capabilities for the next possible disaster or crisis. Some of these efforts have succeeded, but others have faltered or so far proven inadequate.

The United States has also become more interested in reforming its own ability to respond to domestic and overseas crises since the 1990s. The interest in domestic crisis management was fueled by incidents such as the 1993 terrorist attack on the World Trade Center and the domestic terrorist bombing of the Alfred P. Murrah Federal Building in Oklahoma City in 1995. The need to improve its ability to manage complex crises overseas grew largely out of American experiences in Somalia and Haiti, where U.S. officials faced a combination of military/security, economic, and humanitarian assistance challenges. A common theme of crisis management both at home and abroad has been the need to cope more effectively with the effects of a potential use of weapons of mass destruction (WMD), resulting from a growing realization of the magnitude of this particular threat to the United States and its overseas interests. This subcomponent of crisis management, dubbed consequence management, has proven particularly difficult to address in a consistent and comprehensive manner, given the varying nature of the WMD threat and the difficulty of identifying and quickly reacting to the individual agent that may be used (see chapter 2 for a detailed discussion of the terms "crisis management" and "consequence management"). In addition to crisis and consequence management, the United States has also begun to focus on how to prevent and respond to disruptions of critical infrastructures (physical and cyber-based), particularly information and energy infrastructures, both domestically and overseas.

While significant progress had been made in the 1990s identifying the various challenges posed by crisis and consequence management, the legal, organizational, and procedural changes adopted by the United States were fairly modest in scope and, particularly given the change of administrations, remained works in progress when the September 11 attacks occurred. In the wake of these attacks, the United States underwent yet another round of introspection, reorganization, and legislative changes to be better able to detect and prevent a subsequent attack and also to be better able to manage its consequences.

In the spring and summer of 2002, as the new procedures and organizations were found to be wanting, President Bush undertook a wholesale reorganization of the U.S. government on the federal level, creating a new, cabinet-level department with responsibility for homeland security. The new Department of Homeland Security (DHS) essentially came into being in spring 2003. Work also continues within the foreign affairs agencies, the intelligence and law enforcement communities, and the Department of Defense on how the United States can continue to best organize itself for overseas crises, taking into account the new domestic organization and responsibilities. The State Department will remain the lead agency in any overseas emergency (specifically, the U.S. ambassador to a given country, acting as the president's representative), but the picture is less clear at lower levels of international communication and cooperation for other issues of prevention and preparation. Some of these issues might involve, among other activities, the stockpiling and distribution of vaccines, exchange of customs information, interdiction of suspicious cargoes at sea or in the air, and exchange of information of a scientific, legal, information technology (IT) security, business proprietary, or military intelligence nature.

Similarly, Tokyo has made some progress in reorganizing both the national and local levels of government to better address future disasters, crises, and contingencies. The general approach has been to improve the operation of the response system and capabilities that are already available, but not necessarily utilized efficiently or effectively in past crises. While the Japanese government has not gone through the same type of wholesale reorganization that the United States recently undertook for homeland security, it has moved forward on a number of legal, organizational, and procedural reforms that have long been discussed but not implemented. The most dramatic of the recent changes is probably the enactment of a sct of laws (hereafter referred to as "national cmergency legislation") in 2003 concerning Japan's response to a military attack that, among other changes, will help the SDF operate more smoothly in a domestic emergency and strengthen the functions of the Security Council.[2] After these bills were approved by the Diet, Japan's Defense Agency Director Ishiba told reporters, "We now have a scheme of how to respond as a nation in the event of an emergency."[3] He could have easily added the word "finally" to preface his comment, since an early draft form of the legislation was first studied by Prime Minister Takeo Fukuda's cabinet some twenty-six years earlier. Subsequent legislation is planned to create a legal framework for more efficient cooperation between SDF and United States Forces Japan (USFJ) components in the event of an armed attack on Japan, and possibly to create a crisis management agency modeled on FEMA in the United States.[4] Japan's Diet also passed legislation in October 2001 that allowed Japan's SDF to provide non-combat support to the U.S.-led operation Enduring Freedom, which focused on Afghanistan, and authorized the SDF to defend U.S. bases in Japan against possible terrorist attacks.[5] All of these recent changes come on top of earlier reforms such as the establishment of the Cabinet Office for National Security Affairs and Crisis Management (Naikaku Anzen Hoshō/Kiki Kanri Shitsu) in 1998 and the IT Security Office in 2000, as well as the first-ever launching of Japan's own intelligence satellites in 2003.

Basic Differences and Similarities in the U.S. and Japanese Approaches

When considering the expansion of U.S.-Japanese crisis management cooperation, it is important to remember that the two systems for dealing with emergencies and disasters are not cut from the same cloth, and that each has its own special political, cultural, and legal characteristics. One of the most fundamental differences is the relative power and authority of the American president (and the White House) compared with Japan's prime minister (and his Cabinet Office). As will become clear in this monograph, many of the crisis management innovations and reforms in the United States were accomplished through the power of the president's office in the form of presidential decision directives (PDDs) rather than via legislation debated in Congress (although major changes, such as the creation of the DHS, still required action by Congress). In contrast, a majority of organizational changes in Japan, as well as cutting-edge issues involving the SDF, must be drafted in legal language and submitted to the Diet for approval. The Japanese system can still enact major reform measures in this manner, as evidenced by the government administrative restructuring put into effect in January 2001, but the process generally takes longer than it would in the United States and is often subject to greater political compromise as a result.[6]

Compounding the preoccupation in Japan with legal remedies to organizational problems is the educational background of those career bureaucrats who draft the legislation. Most of the high-ranking officials from the Ministry of Foreign Affairs (MOFA), for example, are graduates of the law departments of prestigious Japanese universities. This legal orientation of Japan's policy-making structure and the training of its policy makers is sometimes blamed for the difficulty Japan often encounters in developing clear and coherent policy responses for certain problems. In Japanese policy-making circles, the discussion and eventual remedy quickly become mired in *legal* questions and debates about legal precedents as opposed to a discussion regarding the appropriate *policy* for Japan to adopt.

Other basic differences exist between the two countries that should be highlighted up front. As everyone knows, Japan is a relatively small and densely populated country, squeezing the equivalent of half the U.S. population into an area smaller than the state of California. Government control is more centralized than in the United States. There is a national police agency and a national fire department (as opposed to the myriad of state and local police and fire jurisdictions in the United States), and there is no National Guard equivalent in Japan for prefecture governors to call on in case of emergency (unlike U.S. state governors). Instead, since response to large-scale disasters and similar situations is one of the three primary roles for the SDF, governors in Japan can easily seek the aid of the SDF as needed.[7] It is therefore not uncommon to see SDF personnel and equipment used in large-scale disaster relief exercises, in contrast to the restrictions placed on deploying American military assets domestically under the Posse Comitatus Act.[8] Not all Japanese governors have been quick to call on the SDF, however, in part because of a lack of integrated federal-local disaster relief training (i.e., a few governors simply have not understood well enough how to coordinate activities with the SDF), as well as the dark shadow of the military's role in World War II that still makes some hesitant to involve the SDF.

For these historical reasons, and since Japan's constitution renounces war and limits the SDF to a "defense only" posture, the two countries' militaries have developed a shield-and-sword approach (with SDF as defense and USFJ and other U.S. forces as offense) that dictates the types of assets each can mobilize in the event of an emergency. An example of how this affects crisis management planning is the asymmetry in logistics, airlift, and sealift capabilities. SDF logistical planning is predicated on a defensive mission and relies heavily on the domestic civilian logistics infrastructure (medical, transport and communications, energy, food and water, etc.). The U.S. military, given the multifaceted nature of its mission, is better equipped to supply itself (or perhaps an affected population) in the event of an overseas, offshore, or remote domestic emergency.[9]

Despite all of the differences between the American and Japanese approaches to crisis management, however, the two countries share a great deal in common and have a solid foundation from which to enhance cooperation. Both countries possess vast financial and technical resources and maintain highly trained, well-equipped police, fire, and military forces. Health, medical, and scientific research facilities and personnel are among the most sophisticated and capable in the world. In addition, their crisis management decision-making structures are slowly beginning to look more and more alike, thanks mostly to past and planned reforms in Japan that are finally taking shape, including centralizing decision making and accountability and strengthening the Cabinet Secretariat and Cabinet Office. The United States and Japan also have similar overall ethical codes of conduct and place a high premium on protecting their citizens' civil liberties. The two nations have spent decades cooperating on such undertakings as scientific research projects, business enterprises, military operations, overseas relief and development activities, and intelligence analysis. Enhancing bilateral cooperation in crisis management and consequence management preparation, therefore, would not require a significant amount of effort, but it also cannot simply be expected to happen on its own or derive naturally from other avenues of collaboration. The United States and Japan should each continue to improve their own capabilities, but they should also look to create opportunities for cooperation that can reduce vulnerability, protect and assist their citizens, and strengthen their alliance.

The Case for Cooperation

What has become clear in both Tokyo and Washington throughout the 1990s and the first years of the twenty-first century is that, even with more than a decade of reforms and upgrades, response mechanisms for both national and international crises can still be improved and there is room, and in some cases substantial room, for better collaboration and sharing of lessons learned. There will also be opportunities to operate jointly in certain circumstances. The reasons for this continuing need to collaborate and reform are threefold.

First, crises of the type seen in past decade, and likely into the future, cross bureaucratic boundaries vertically and horizontally. No single government agency at the national level has either the mandate or the capabilities on its own to cope with crises such as large-scale earthquakes, terrorist attacks, cyber attacks, or cross-border epidemics. In addition, responsibilities for detection, prevention, and response reside not just at the national level but also at lower levels of governmental authority, whether they are state/prefecture or town and city. Moreover, an international alliance of government-affiliated agencies and organizations will be particularly important in the detection and prevention of many man-made crises (such as terrorist attacks or accidents involving oil supertankers, nuclear facilities, or cruise ships).

Second, crises that are often seen as national in scope in fact have international dimensions, and such dimensions can quickly develop as situations evolve. A massive earthquake in Tokyo, for example, will affect tens of thousands of Americans living and working there, as well as American businesses, the Japanese economy as a whole, and the regional economy. U.S. military forces in Japan also will have their operations disrupted. In a similar vein, the September 11 attacks resulted in the deaths of nationals from many countries. Air traffic to and from the United States was halted, affecting economies and government operations in other countries – including Japan's primary gateway to the United States, the New Tokyo International Airport in Narita. The SARS outbreak in 2003 negatively affected the economies of several nations and cities. Attacks on information infrastructures can also quickly become international, as has been shown by frequent debilitating viruses and worms on the Internet. These are just a few examples of how major crises can transcend borders and affect a region or broader international communities.

Third, large-scale crises, natural or man-made, can often overwhelm the response capabilities of the affected country, even if they are perfectly prepared and coordinated. The United States and Japan, the two largest economies in the world, cannot each necessarily cope with disasters or crises alone. This is particularly true if they are responding to requests for help in a third country. In countries with fewer capabilities and resources, the problems will only be exacerbated. The scope of future threats, whether they involve international terrorists as in the September 11 attacks or cyber attacks that could have an outsized impact on high-technology societies such as the United States and Japan, is another reason for increased cooperation and collaboration between the two allies.

The increase in scope and intensity of natural disasters and man-made crises argues for international cooperation generally, but the United States and Japan – as long-standing partners in what is widely recognized as the most important bilateral security relationship and seen as such in both capitals – have a unique relationship that suggests even more extensive exchanges and cooperative efforts between them. Both the size and the interconnectedness of the U.S. and Japanese economies make the impact of large-scale crises involving either one of them immediately international in scope. Even using the less generous measurement of purchasing-power parity, the United States and Japan account for almost one-third of world gross domestic product (GDP). Add a dozen other large economies in the world (such as China, India, South Korea, Brazil, and some EU members), and together they would represent nearly three-quarters of global production. Cooperation among a relatively small number of countries can therefore have a tremendous impact worldwide, and the United States and Japan (together with the European Union) have a unique opportunity to lead. In terms of trade, Japan is third after Canada and Mexico as a market for U.S. exports, and it is the leading market for U.S. agricultural exports. It is also the third leading supplier of U.S. imports, and the United States is Japan's number-one trading partner. The two countries are the world's largest consumers of oil (about one-third of global consumption combined) and the largest oil importers.[10]

The vast majority of this trade takes place through ocean shipping, although certain high-value items use air transport. In addition to cargo, passenger traffic between the two countries is enormous. In 2000, Japan was among the top five international gateways for passenger travel to and from the United States (the others were the United Kingdom, Canada, Mexico, and Germany). After London-Heathrow, Tokyo is the largest gateway city for passenger travel to the United States. Connections of this sort, when linked with the growing and changing nature of threats to countries – from terrorism to communicable diseases – point to an area of focus for joint interest and common efforts. Finally, in the financial realm, New York and Tokyo are two of the top five financial hubs in the world, and the interconnectivity of global finance means that the United States and Japan have an intricate interdependence on the world capital markets. Japan is one of the largest sources of foreign portfolio capital and foreign direct investment in the United States, and the United States is the largest source of foreign portfolio and direct investments in Japan.

In addition, the large presence of U.S. military forces on Japanese territory means that disasters and crises in Japan will have an impact on U.S. military capabilities and readiness, not only to conduct operations in support of the U.S.-Japan treaty obligations but also on a regional and indeed global scale. The United States has more than eighty facilities in Japan supporting missions by the Department of Defense, the State Department, and the intelligence community. Some of these are solely U.S. facilities. Others are shared with the Japanese government, such as the U.S. Fleet Activities base at Sasebo in Kyushu. These facilities all rely, to varying degrees, on Japanese critical infrastructures (electricity, phone lines, and other utilities) to operate. The United States and Japan have an interest in insuring that these facilities are protected against attacks and operate to the full level of their efficiency, particularly during contingencies that affect the interests of these two countries. U.S. Pacific Command (PACOM) and USFJ also represent a well-trained and well-equipped resource on which Japan can rely if needed.

Moreover, certain types of crises could be triggered by the fact that the United States maintains military forces in Japan, for example should they become the target of terrorist attacks. Japan itself could also become the target of an attack as it assumes a higher profile in such efforts as reconstruction in Iraq, policing against WMD proliferation, or similar tasks related to the GWOT in the future. Indeed, an audiotape purportedly from terrorist leader Osama bin Laden that aired in October 2003 specifically mentioned Japan as a target for retaliation, one of only eight nations so mentioned.[11] If Aum Shinrikyo and Al Qaeda are any indication, there is also a desire on the part of these types of groups to cause ever larger numbers of casualties and greater destruction per attack. Both the Tokyo subway sarin attack and intelligence recovered from Al Qaeda camps in Afghanistan indicate that terrorist groups are utilizing WMD as well as actively seeking them. The focus on WMD in a traditional war setting, therefore, has had to be expanded to responding to its use in a non-traditional setting such as a terrorist attack on civilian targets.

As will be noted in the case study on critical infrastructure protection, global reliance on critical infrastructures, and on the cyber infrastructures that increasingly support them, is continually growing. The United States and Japan are at the forefront of this trend, and therefore are most likely to be targeted and have the potential to suffer the greatest amount of damage from a successful attack. While the global evolution of dependence on cyberspace is even more difficult to track, most estimates are that it will increase – not only in advanced countries but also in those countries just crossing the digital divide. These newly "wired" countries, however, are the least likely to have taken the time or expended the resources to make their networks secure. Given the nature of the Internet, that means that countries such as the United States and Japan – even if they focus significant effort on security – will in many ways be only as secure as the weakest link to which they are connected. This phenomenon argues not only for national efforts, but also for broader and deeper international cooperative efforts to address the issue of cyber security.

By stepping up cooperation with the United States, Japan has an opportunity to make better use of the U.S.-Japan alliance to complement its own resources, to help prevent or deter a man-made crisis, and to enhance its ability to deal with the consequences of a potential major catastrophe for the benefit of its own people. For the United States, increased cooperation with Japan will not only more effectively extend its perimeter of preparedness and provide access to the experience and expertise resident in Japan, but it will also demonstrate to the Japanese people a practical, positive contribution of the U.S.-Japan alliance to their everyday lives and enhance the base-hosting environment in support of America's own national and regional security objectives.

There is, of course, a strong domestic component to improving U.S.-Japan crisis management cooperation, as each country is (and should be) primarily focused on improving its own domestic capabilities. Here then, the "cooperative" actions would be the regular exchange of information regarding lessons learned and updating each other on the nuances of domestic reform. There are, however, bilateral and multilateral components to crisis management cooperation as well. Bilateral cooperation mostly takes the form of joint planning and training to respond to certain situations either in Japan or surrounding areas. There might also be opportunities for Japan to aid the United States in the case of earthquakes, volcanic eruptions, nuclear power problems, or other situations in which Japan has special expertise. The multilateral component represents an opportunity for the United States and Japan to coordinate their contributions to, and in some cases take leadership of, international efforts to prevent and manage different types of crises. Examples of the kinds of crises that would benefit from a multilateral response include cyber security, epidemic disease, massive oil spills or other major accidents, financial meltdowns, terrorist attacks, and natural disasters in poorer countries unable to deal with the consequences.

U.S.-Japan crisis management cooperation is not a panacea that will solve the world's ills and protect against all catastrophes. It is simply a prudent step already being undertaken, but one that can be more effectively focused and executed. Dramatic change is taking place in both countries and in the international community with regard to crisis and consequence management strategies, investment, and organization. Now is the right time to design into the new structures and procedures the appropriate patterns of cooperation that can serve both countries' interests. In order to do this effectively, it is important to develop a common understanding about the context and details of the changes taking place in both nations and to jointly identify the most promising targets for mutually beneficial cooperation. Contributing to this effort is the purpose of this monograph.

Summary of Policy Recommendations

To help U.S. and Japanese policy makers take advantage of the crisis and consequence management opportunities that accompany the dramatic change taking place in both countries, the project organizers have developed a "one-two-three" approach that could help facilitate cooperation and maximize its benefits. This approach is a simple way to express how the United States and Japan might go about building a shared framework for enhancing crisis and consequence management cooperation for both countries' advantage. Details of the project's policy recommendations can be found in chapter 5.

The one-two-three approach begins with each nation identifying *one* primary point of contact or coordinator for crisis and consequence management issues. It continues with a focus on *two* categories of primary targets or priorities for cooperation (bilateral and multilateral), and on *three* methods of cooperation (exchanges, exercises, and strategic planning). This approach could be useful in helping the allies keep track of how they cooperate and making sure that each agency or department understands how its activities relate to a larger scheme of cooperative efforts. Cooperation in the field of crisis and consequence management is, by its nature, diverse and involves many different scenarios and actors. It does not need to be tightly controlled, but it can be more effectively coordinated and implemented.

The key to realizing the benefits of cooperation in this area is to integrate crisis and consequence management into existing alliance structures, rather than add a new layer of issues to the agenda. The simplest way to achieve this would be for each country to explicitly identify one primary point of contact or coordinator for U.S.-Japan crisis and consequence management cooperation, drawing on the work of the other departments and ministries. For the United States, the American Embassy in Tokyo could easily serve as the primary nexus for this aspect of bilateral cooperation, given its central role in any crisis involving the two countries (probably an assistant to the U.S. deputy chief of mission). To supplement this government point of contact, the project recommends encouraging the American business community to create a similar position so that views from the private sector can be incorporated into official discussions of crisis and consequence management policies and cooperation (ideally within the American Chamber of Commerce in Japan). On the Japan side of the equation, the most likely counterparts would be the Cabinet Secretariat (an assistant to the deputy chief cabinet secretary for crisis management or a particular assistant chief cabinet secretary) and the business lobby Nippon Keidanren.

As a part of this process, the two countries need to agree on a relatively small set of clear priorities that can supplement bilateral and multilateral work already taking place. On the bilateral front, priority areas for cooperation include certain Japan-based catastrophic events, such as a massive earthquake or a significant nuclear accident. An additional bilateral contingency for which the allies should consider planning is a missile attack by North Korea on Japan, particularly one that involves a chemical or nuclear weapon. Priorities in the multilateral arena are already emerging, and a recent action plan agreed to at a meeting of the Asia Pacific Economic Cooperation (APEC) in October 2003 touches on many of them. The plan focuses on countering terrorism, and it addresses enhancing secure trade, halting terrorist financing, and promoting cyber security, energy security, and the health of communities. This is an appropriate short list from which U.S.-Japan cooperation on multilateral initiatives can begin, but there is no need for the issues to be seen only through a lens of countering terrorism or for limiting discussion to APEC. Oil spills, nuclear waste issues, controlling epidemic diseases, and similar non-terrorist-related challenges can also be discussed in this context.

The United States and Japan can, and should, continue to cooperate in bilateral and multilateral forums in three basic ways. The first is through information exchanges, which involve an organized and concerted effort to understand each other's capabilities, laws, procedures, and learning of lessons as each pursues its own governmental and societal effort to plan for and help prevent crises. The second set of efforts should be planning and exercising to assist in certain situations drawn from the priorities identified above. Finally, and overarching this cooperation on the ground, the United States and Japan should conduct regular, strategic planning discussions at a relatively high level on these issues to continually shape the agenda, monitor progress, and coordinate strategy on the multilateral front. Specific recommendations, and the rationale for pursuing them, are presented in chapter 5.

Notes for Chapter One

1   "Prime Minister Junichiro Koizumi's indication that his Liberal Democratic Party intends to draft an amendment to the Constitution by November 2005 will constitute a major turning point in the nation's constitutional debate. Koizumi also revealed a plan to implement legislation on calling a national referendum, which is a necessary precondition to amending the Constitution…LDP Secretary General Taku Yamasaki pointed out the need to amend the Constitution in a speech Monday, using North Korean missiles as an example. 'Even if it becomes clear that [North Korea] intends to launch a missile, Japan can't launch a counterattack because of Article 9 of the Constitution,' he said." *Yomiuri Shimbun* (in Japanese), "Constitution Key Poll Issue / Koizumi's Push for Draft by 2005 to be Focus of Elections," August 27, 2003.

2   The three so-called national emergency bills (*yūji hōsei*) are, individually, the Law Concerning Measures to Ensure National Independence and Security in a Situation of Armed Attack; the Law to Amend the Self-Defense Forces Law; and the Law to Amend the Security Council Establishment Law. Japan's House of Councilors passed the legislation on June 6, 2003.

3   Mari Yamaguchi, "Japan Expands Military's Right to Fight," Associated Press, June 6, 2003.

4   "Japan Brief: Diet Enacts Three National Emergency Bills," Foreign Press Center/Japan, June 2003.

5   Known as the Anti-Terrorism Special Measures Law, this legislation was passed by the House of Councilors on October 29, 2001.

6   For a discussion of the administrative reform process in Japan that led to the government reorganization in 2001, see Tomohito Shinoda, *Leading Japan: The Role of the Prime Minister* (Westport, Conn.: Praeger Publishers, 2000), 183-200. Passage of the Anti-Terrorism Special Measures Law in October 2001 (in response to the terrorist attacks in the United States a month earlier) is a notable exception to the normally slow pace of change in Japan, though it should be remembered that this legislation is temporary and has a sunset provision.

7   As described in "Japan's National Defense Program Outline In
     and After Fiscal Year 1996," *Japan Ministry of Foreign Affairs Official
     Web Site*, http://www.infojapan.org/policy/security/defense96/
     index.html. The other two stated primary roles for the SDF are de-
     fense of the country and contribution to building a more stable
     security environment (via international peace cooperation activ-
     ities and international disaster relief operations, participation in
     security dialogues and other confidence building measures, with
     an emphasis on arms control and disarmament).

8   The Posse Comitatus Act was originally passed in 1878 and has
     been amended over the years. It limits the ability of U.S. military
     organizations to deploy forces domestically, to search and seize
     property, to make arrests, and to conduct domestic surveillance
     and other domestic "policing" activities. The act is not completely
     restrictive, however, and U.S. troops have been deployed in border
     patrol duties, for drug trafficking interdiction, as well as to assist
     with security at the 2002 Olympic Winter Games in Salt Lake City,
     Utah.

9   Japan's SDF recently proposed a major reorganization that would
     partly address the perceived insufficiencies of its logistics and
     communications capabilities. The plan is to improve the "jointness"
     by creating an integrated branch charged with logistics, commu-
     nications, and other support activities of the SDF's three branches
     (air, maritime, ground), which are now being carried out sepa-
     rately by each branch. Tetsuo Hidaka, "Defense Agency Proposes
     Logistics Branch for SDF," *The Daily Yomiuri*, September 9, 2003.

10   Central Intelligence Agency, *The World Factbook 2003*,
     http://www.cia.gov/cia/publications/factbook/index.html.

11   John J. Lumpkin, "Bin Laden Tape Likely Authentic, CIA Says," As-
     sociated Press News Service, October 20, 2003.

CHAPTER TWO

Understanding Crisis & Consequence Management in Both Countries

❖

When dealing with a binational, bilingual situation in which the stakes are high and decision time limited, getting language right and clearly understanding each other is extremely important. The scope of this challenge has been demonstrated in numerous bilateral planning sessions, where fortunately there is plenty of time to clear up any miscommunications. A typical example occurred at a recent U.S.-Japan joint session to develop a coordinated plan (*keikaku*) involving certain SDF actions that could only be carried out with special approval of the Diet. In Japanese, the word *keikaku* means "plan" but it also has a connotation of "intention" or a sense that the plan is to be implemented. Some senior Japanese officials began to balk at finalizing the plan because they did not want to commit to a set of actions for which they did not have full authority. Among other worries, the Japanese thought that the United States might expect that these joint actions were agreed to and could be carried out on a moment's notice. The Americans in the room explained their view that a plan is independent of the political decision (and in some cases the legal interpretation) to act. A U.S. plan to deploy tactical nuclear weapons on a given battlefield, to use an extreme example, certainly does not mean that such action is either likely or even plausible; it is just a plan. After much discussion and several phone calls to senior officials in both countries, the Japanese eventually felt comfortable that the Americans understood the political and legal context under which the plan would be developed, and they continued working on the project.[12] This anecdote highlights not only the importance of joint planning and exercises to clear up misunderstandings before a crisis occurs, but also the need to take time to understand each other's definitions and basic views of the issues under discussion. This chapter clarifies the meaning of crisis management and consequence management in American and Japanese contexts and explains how this research project addressed the issue.

In the United States

The U.S. and global response to the September 11 attacks illustrated crisis and consequence management in action as well as the need for both to be able to proceed simultaneously. When the attacks occurred, the United States responded on two separate, but related, tracks. The first track was the **consequence management** response: local (city), state, and federal authorities responded to the damage caused by the attacks, seeking to help victims, assessing the damage, and restoring necessary services to the areas affected. This involved local fire, police, and emergency medical teams as well as hospitals and specialized military units. These last units were sent in to detect whether the attacks had involved anything more than conventional explosives. Most of the units responding in New York, Washington, and Pennsylvania followed long-established rules and procedures in place for large-scale natural disasters: readying for mass casualties, looking for victims in collapsed buildings, and battling large-scale fires. In essence, their protocols were developed for what had previously been termed "emergency management" or "disaster response" within the United States.

The second track, happening simultaneously on September 11, was crisis response, or **crisis management:** efforts to deter and protect against further attacks and efforts to find perpetrators or their backers both in the United States and abroad. At first, these involved a number of immediate and short-term actions such as the grounding of all air traffic in the United States, the diversion of all in-bound international air traffic toward the United States, and pursuit of various leads on the ground to discover whether there were additional terrorists who were in the middle of trying to hijack more airplanes. Over time, the U.S. response also involved diplomatic, intelligence, law enforcement, and military activities against the Al Qaeda terrorist network, once it was identified as the attacker, and against the Taliban governing group in Afghanistan, once it was determined that it was harboring Al Qaeda's leadership.

The consequence management portion of the response effort drew on more long-standing disaster response preparation and training at both the local and federal level, but the novel terminology – consequence management – and its focus on the potential for an incident to have involved WMD is relatively recent in the United States. Interestingly, the new attention paid to the needs for this type of response dates largely from the use of WMD in Japan – the sarin poison gas attack in Tokyo – and from a conventional bomb in the United States – the Oklahoma City attack. In 1995, U.S. President Bill Clinton signed PDD 39, covering the terrorist use of WMD. In that document, the potential for terrorist use of WMD was divided into two categories: domestic and international. In each category, response was also divided into two categories: crisis response and consequence management. Crisis response comprises those counter-terrorist activities conducted once a specific threat by terrorists to use WMD has been identified or if an actual incident has taken place. Crisis management in this context, therefore, encompasses all of the operations taken to prevent an incident after a WMD threat has been made, seeking out and/or arresting perpetrators to save lives, as well as ongoing procedures to prevent perpetration of additional terrorist actions after an event has occurred.

The American concept of crisis management applies to more than just WMD threats, of course, though perhaps the term is sometimes used in a confusingly broad manner. The terminology has its roots in the Cuban missile crisis of 1962, when the primary focus was on mitigating an escalating confrontation that could lead to nuclear war. Today, the term "crisis" is used in various situations, such as the taking of hostages, financial meltdowns, shortages of a vital resource, or outbreaks of contagious diseases. Traditionally, however, a "crisis" involves a high possibility of military hostilities, essentially a dilemma of peace or war, and it generally involves as well a series of important turning points in a sequence of events accompanied by a sense of urgency, stress, and increased time pressure.

Immediate access to accurate, vital information and quick decision making are critical to effective crisis management. A streamlined process of two-way communication is important, as is planning for a variety of crises and gaming out possible responses in advance. This monograph accepts a somewhat expansive definition of crisis management to include events other than military action, for the simple fact that many kinds of crises can cause serious harm to human security if not quickly contained. Moreover, although U.S.-Japan military cooperation in crisis situations is important, there are legal and political reasons why non-military avenues of cooperation will at times be easier to accomplish (and will help prepare the ground for subsequent military cooperation). The focus of the project, therefore, is on situations that risk escalation and significant damage to people, property, businesses, and the environment, and where bilateral or multilateral cooperation can improve response effectiveness. Managing this risk could involve military and/or non-military responses, including diplomacy, intelligence gathering, and coordinating adjustments to energy, IT, travel, financial, trade, or other kinds of infrastructure, as well as other measures.

The primary objectives of consequence management are 1) early decontamination and medical treatment to ensure the survival of the maximum number of people; 2) containment; 3) cleanup and disposal of contaminated material and debris; 4) reestablishment of self-sufficiency and essential services; 5) repair or replacement of damaged infrastructure; and 6) resumption of economic activities. The September 11 attacks required all of the areas of consequence management to be addressed other than decontamination (though decontamination was a part of the response to the post-September 11 anthrax mailings in the United States). Detection operations were carried out to determine if WMD were present at any of the three attack sites, but in all other respects the operations on the consequence management side paralleled those of a large-scale natural disaster and most of the points above. In contemporary U.S. parlance, consequence management generally refers to a response to an NBC event (either accidental or deliberate), but this monograph will also include reactions to large-scale natural disasters as a form of consequence management for the purposes of discussion, given the similarities in the personnel and methods of responding. In addition, with the presence of U.S. military forces in Japan and in the region, and because U.S. and Japanese non-governmental organizations (NGOs) are beginning to collaborate more regularly, there are several opportunities to cooperate on certain consequence management situations in Japan and throughout Asia that bear further exploration.

The distinction in the United States between the two areas of operational responsibility, domestic and foreign, helps to determine which agency is in charge of the scene and what types of capabilities are needed. In domestic situations, the division in responsibilities is between law enforcement – if there is the potential that perpetrators are still present or if a crime needs to be investigated – and disaster relief, where the focus is on assisting victims and cleaning up from the event. The level of government involvement – local, state, and/or federal – is determined primarily by the severity of the incident and where specialized capabilities reside to deal with crisis or consequence management needs. Similarly, the involvement of the U.S. military in support of civilian authorities depends upon the scope of the incident and the specialized capabilities required. When incidents occur outside of the United States, the division between the two concepts remains intact, but different government agencies take the lead, with the State Department having primary liaison responsibility with the host government to determine the appropriate role for U.S. agencies. The evolution, particularly since September 11, of U.S. organizational structures and responsibilities for both crisis and consequence management is detailed in chapter 4.

In Japan

In Japan, the terminology for responding to crises is not bifurcated as it is in the United States. The Japanese government uses "crisis administration/management" (*kiki kanri*) to encompass political-military and/or law enforcement contingencies as well as natural disasters (though, as will be shown later, the potential military component has historically been deemphasized). This generalized definition is not due to an inability to be more precise. Rather, it is the result of two elements in Japanese geography and politics. The first is simply the fact that geography and geology make Japan a country highly susceptible to earthquakes, so the crisis-planning focus has been on preparing for and responding to these potentially devastating events. The second is more a matter of perception, namely that some in Japan remain reluctant to highlight that crises may have a military component to them – either in cause or in response – because of Japan's World War II legacy and constitutional restrictions. As one example, certain segments of the Japanese polity tend to equate the use of the term "emergency" (*hijō jitai*) with martial law situations before and during World War II.[13]

It is how these terms are ultimately translated into organizational structure and public understanding, however, that is most important, and in this respect Japan's sensitivities to its militaristic past have made it slow to fully integrate the civilian and military sides of crisis planning. In theory, the term *kiki kanri*, when it is applied to government efforts, is supposed to be aimed at securing "the lives and properties of the Japanese National," as described in Article 15 of the Cabinet Law. Conceptually speaking, therefore, *kiki kanri* encompasses the entire range of crisis situations, from natural disasters to international security or national defense matters. What tends to happen, however, is a more compartmentalized approach that results in less than ideal interaction among the various offices. The responsible department in the cabinet used to be called the Cabinet

Office for National Security Affairs and Crisis Management, in an effort to link the two kinds of crises, but jurisdictionally the jobs were divided, where the former was headed by MOFA and the Defense Agency and the latter by the National Police Agency (NPA), without a strong unifying role of the prime minister. Today, the official lead for this function is the deputy chief cabinet secretary for crisis management, who, as of this writing, is a member of the NPA organization. In the response part of the equation then, Japan's SDF has had perhaps an underweighted role in planning for or responding to crises in Japan (despite the fact that consequence management has become one of the SDF's three core functions).

Any government is wise to resist the casual use of military assets during peacetime. Local and civil authorities should always be the first line of defense, but it is also prudent for governments to prepare for and practice the responsible deployment of certain military capabilities when requested. In Japan, while there is a legal framework for employing the SDF to support other agencies – for example the NPA – with the approval of the prime minister, the use of the SDF in peacetime emergencies has for quite some time needed more methodical consideration. The issue gets particularly sensitive when command and control questions are raised. There are potential cases when the Maritime SDF might assist and coordinate with the Coast Guard to thwart an intruder or monitor a dangerous situation, and in extreme cases the SDF can exercise an element of control over the Coast Guard if the intruder is too heavily armed. With regard to the NPA, however, the SDF can communicate and cooperate with, but not command, NPA personnel. This is appropriate, but it emphasizes the need for clarity in roles and responsibilities that is being addressed, in part, by the national emergency legislation.

A telling example of the difference between *having* the means to respond to a crisis and *using* those means occurred during Prime Minister Toshiki Kaifu's administration during the first Gulf War in 1990. Even though the Cabinet Office for National Security Affairs (Naikaku Anzen Hoshō Shitsu) had been created a few years earlier to improve the coordination and handling of important national security situations, the prime minister failed to label the Gulf crisis as a "significant emergency" and left management of the issue in the hands of MOFA. This decision consequently limited the executive office's ability to lead the response directly and contributed to Japan's poorly rated handling of the situation.[14] The problem was in part a reluctance to invoke certain sensitive language and in part the result of bureaucratic infighting. When the office was originally proposed (primarily to correct perceived shortcomings during the aftermath of the tragic downing of flight KAL 007 in 1983), Japan's MOFA and Defense Agency strongly opposed the idea for fear that it might intrude on their jurisdictions, and they fought to limit the office's sphere of authority.[15] This kind of history and dynamics of bureaucratic reform are important to keep in mind as Japan continues to move toward a centralization of crisis management functions within the Cabinet Secretariat and Cabinet Office (and possibly the eventual creation of a full-fledged crisis management agency). Overcoming compartmentalized, jurisdictional divisions in evolving bureaucratic organizations is a near-term challenge for both Japan and the United States.

This bureaucratic resistance to centralization and the general reluctance to use certain language, however, is wavering in Japan. The national emergency legislation (mentioned in chapter 1) that was recently passed by the Diet is a sign of this trend, though the new legislation only relates to the use of the SDF in the context of an armed attack on Japan, and not the broader use of these forces in a range of crises. There are also a number of theoretical debates about the laws with regard to what constitutes an "armed attack" or one that is "imminent" (e.g., does a missile attack count, or apparent preparations for a launch?), and these will need to be clarified over the next few Diet sessions. Moreover, no consensus has yet been reached regarding the degree to which the prime minister should be allowed to assume some of the prefectural governors' authority during a crisis to carry out such tasks as ordering evacuations of citizens, managing the disbursement of aid, and ordering doctors, nurses, truckers, gas station attendants, and other workers to continue operations under dangerous conditions. The preference is for central government authorities to consult with local officials and then let local officials implement the decisions, but there might not always be time for this process of consultation. In addition, the national emergency legislation does not include detailed provisions for cooperation with U.S. forces in case of a military emergency in Japan. During debate over the bills defense chief Ishiba said, "It is important to give a legal guarantee allowing U.S. forces to act in an emergency situation as soon as possible."[16] All of these issues will be discussed in the next few years, and a special state minister has been given this overall portfolio.[17]

Linked to this discussion is an issue that bears mention, though it is not the focus of this project or monograph: Japan's right to, and exercise of, collective self-defense. A brief explanation is useful since the issue is inextricably linked to some of the crisis management proposals under consideration. Japan has long interpreted the war-renouncing article in its constitution to mean that Japan possesses the right to defend itself militarily, but that this self-defense capability (the size, composition, and actions of its armed forces) must be limited to the "minimum necessary level." The issue is relevant because successive administrations in Japan have consequently interpreted this to mean that although the country has a right (under international law) to exercise collective self-defense (that is, the right to use force to stop an armed attack on a foreign country with which it has close relations), Japan cannot exercise this right because of its interpretation of domestic law (since collective self-defense would exceed this minimum necessary level).[18] This explains why Japanese officials are constantly doing legal somersaults when certain types of U.S.-Japan defense cooperation issues are raised, be they development and ultimate operation of a missile defense system, certain joint exercises at sea, or operations in a third country. For domestic legal reasons, therefore, SDF actions must either be clearly in defense of Japan or clearly in support of international peace and security initiatives (another acceptable use of SDF assets if under United Nations' (UN) auspices, such as peacekeeping in Cambodia and East Timor). This fact will complicate the allies' efforts to expand bilateral crisis management cooperation in a predominately military-to-military context outside of these two categories, so it will be important to explore other, non-military opportunities for cooperation as well.

It is also worth briefly explaining how government officials classify different kinds of crises, because this will allow the two countries to focus on those crises for which cooperation can be the most productive. The United States and Japan use a similar system for classifying crises. Broadly speaking, crises and disasters are classified as either natural or man-made, with man-made crises further divided into intentional crises (a terrorist attack of some kind) or unintentional crises (an accident at a nuclear power plant, for example, or a large oil spill). Intentional and unintentional crises are also sometimes referred to as incidents and accidents, respectively.

These distinctions can be important, since although the mechanics of cleaning up an oil spill or putting out a large forest fire do not depend on whether or not they were intentionally caused, future prevention of similar incidents will require special expertise and investigative actions if they were, in fact, malicious. Since the United States and Japan are two of the world's largest makers and consumers of products made by humans, it is natural that U.S.-Japan cooperation would focus on man-made crises. With the exception of a massive earthquake in Japan, a naturally occurring, cross-border health epidemic, or a joint response to a natural disaster in a third country, there is less need for the two countries to spend time and energy thinking how best to respond jointly to a natural disaster. In the area of man-made crises, however, there are plenty of oppor-

Crisis Classification for Preparing Response Plans

natural disaster
- earthquake
- tidal wave
- wind and water damage (dike break, high tide, etc.,)
- volcanic damage

incident
- hijack
- terrorism by WMD

accident
- passenger boat accident
- oil spill
- aviation accident
- railway accident (with many human injuries/deaths)
- road accident
- refinery accident
- large fire
- nuclear accident

tunities and incentives to pool resources and talents for more effective responses and, perhaps of greater importance, to enhance prevention. Specific kinds of incidents and accidents on which the United States and Japan should concentrate include those involving critical infrastructure, such as energy, transportation, financial, and IT networks. The potential for hostile military or terrorist activity in the Asian region is of particular concern, especially that involving the use of missiles and/or NBC agents or weapons.

The next two chapters examine in greater detail how crisis management and consequence management planning has evolved in the United States and Japan, and on how these processes, procedures, and capabilities might evolve in the future. In chapter 3, four case studies are examined, with a focus on how they have affected, or might affect, each country's policies on crisis and consequence management. In chapter 4, the evolution of both the threats and the responses potentially requiring more effective crisis and consequence management in each country is detailed and compared across crises and between the two countries. The various threats that have arisen and may arise in the United States, Japan, and areas of joint interest to the two allies are also examined. The evolution of crisis and consequence management laws, plans, procedures, and organizations are then discussed with an eye to teasing out areas of common interest, common problems, and common or competing approaches to preferred solutions. In the final chapter of this study, the scope for cooperation and collaboration between the United States and Japan – as they move forward to improve their crisis and consequence management capabilities – is examined. This collaboration may take the form of exchanges of information and views, actual joint endeavors to plan for and assist in responding to crises in each of the two countries, exercises to improve cooperative approaches, research and development to improve the technological components of crisis and consequence management, and outreach efforts to assist third countries in their planning and preparation for both avoiding and responding to future crises on their territories.

Notes for Chapter Two

12 Story related by two Japanese participants in separate personal interviews, August 2003. Official Japanese government publications often use a phonetic spelling of the English word manual instead of the Japanese word *keikaku* when discussing response plans to indicate that they are more or less generic. The word *keikaku* is generally reserved for individual cases to be discussed and approved by the government in response to each crisis or incident.

13 Perhaps for this reason, in Japan "emergency situation" is generally referred to as *kinkyu jitai* in government publications (e.g., in Japan defense white papers), thus avoiding the historical nuance of *hijo jitai*.

14 Shinoda, *Leading Japan: The Role of the Prime Minister*, 75. As another example of Japan's past aversion to the military, in 1986 the Cabinet Office for National Security Affairs was meant to support the Security Council of Japan, which at that time was composed of the prime minister and five cabinet ministers, among them the Economic Planning Agency's director general but not the Defense Agency's chief. Today the Security Council of Japan includes the Defense Agency's director general, evidence of changing attitudes to the military in Japan.

15 Ibid., as told by Masaharu Gotoda (chief cabinet secretary to Prime Minister Nakasone) in his memoir.

16 Nao Shimoyachi, "Bill on U.S. Cooperation in Attack Needed: Ishiba," *Japan Times*, May 17, 2003. Although this article used the English word "guarantee," a better word might be "provision," since the fundamental guarantee of U.S. support is essentially codified in Article 5 of the U.S.-Japan Security Treaty.

17 State minister for disaster management and national emergency legislation. The emergency legislation component of this minister's portfolio was first added in the September 2003 cabinet re-shuffle.

18 Japan Defense Agency, "The Basic Concept of Japan's Defense Policy," *Defense of Japan 2002*, chapter 2, section 1, translated by Urban Connections (Tokyo, 2002).

CHAPTER THREE

Case Studies in Crisis & Consequence Management

✣

In each of the case studies in this chapter, a similar set of questions and issues is explored in order to provide a basis for comparing Japanese and U.S. crises, perceptions of crises, responses, lessons, and plans for the future. The questions revolve around the nature of the crisis, the response, and lessons learned so far by governments and analysts. The first series of questions is about the nature of the crisis and whether it was anticipated or planned for in general. If so, then the second area of analysis is on how well the planned response met the requirements and how well the plan was executed. If not, the analysis looks at why the crisis was not anticipated and planned for and what factors contributed to this lack of preparedness. The final series of questions concerns specific shortfalls identified, lessons learned, and whether and how those lessons have so far been applied in preparations for future crises of this or similar types.

Kobe/Hanshin Earthquake

The Disaster

On the morning of January 17, 1995, a massive earthquake measuring 7.2 on the Richter scale unexpectedly struck Hyogo Prefecture in the Hanshin region of west-central Japan. The event, officially called the Great Hanshin-Awaji Earthquake but frequently referred to as the Kobe earthquake after the city in the region that experienced the greatest damage, was Japan's worst natural disaster in almost seventy years. Hyogo Prefecture is the eighth-largest of Japan's forty-seven prefectures, with about 5.5 million people, including more than 1.5 million in the capital city of Kobe. Kobe is a port city and an important industrial center in Japan. The broader Kansai region accounts for some 19 percent of Japan's gross domestic product (with a GDP greater than that of Canada or Spain).[19] The port of Kobe is one of Japan's largest and, before the earthquake, ranked sixth in the world, handling roughly 12 percent of Japanese exports.[20]

The earthquake resulted in over sixty-four hundred deaths and forty thousand reported injuries. About 240,000 houses were partially or completely destroyed, forcing more than 315,000 people to flee their neighborhoods. The quake severely damaged Kobe's water system (near total city-wide failure, leaving about 1.3 million households without water), exacerbating the problem caused by fires. Full water service was not restored

The Kansai Region of Japan

until ninety-one days after the earthquake. In addition, other utility services were severely affected: 1.1 million residents lost electricity (seven days till restoration), 860,000 lost natural-gas service (eighty-five days), and 300,000 were without phone service (fifteen days). The loss of telecom services had an adverse impact on response timeliness and effectiveness. Over 150 fires broke out, killing thousands, contributing significantly to the casualty total, and destroying many of the buildings and houses.[21] The direct damage caused by the quake has been estimated at between $80 billion and $150 billion, depending on how one calculates (for example, value of assets lost versus cost to replace), though even the higher figure does not include indirect economic effects from loss of life, business interruption, and loss of production. Close to $90 billion was expended by the Japanese public sector in post-quake recovery efforts.[22] The scope of the disaster highlighted the impact upon people and infrastructure and how damage to the latter can diminish the effectiveness of responses, no matter how well thought out and planned.

Japanese Planning and Preparedness

As one would expect given Japan's geography and history with natural disasters, the earthquake was not unanticipated in the general sense. Japan, over centuries, has had to cope with earthquakes, floods, tsunamis, and other natural disasters. The Great Kanto Earthquake of 1923 was huge in terms of magnitude (thought to be 8.0 on the Richter scale), and it wiped out close to one-third of Tokyo. The modern legal framework for managing disasters on a national basis, including responding to earthquakes, began with the 1961 Disaster Countermeasures Basic Act. Each of the major central government ministries in Japan has a part to play in disaster planning and response, and a national-level coordinating body in the cabinet – the Central Disaster Prevention Council (Chūō Bōsai Kaigi, or CDPC) – is assigned to coordinate these activities among the various ministries (a critical function given the complexity of inter-ministry communication). In addition, this policy planning and coordination mechanism is supplemented by a more operationally oriented body, the Headquarters for Disaster Countermeasures (Saigai Taisaku Honbu, or HDC), that is supposed to be established once a disaster actually occurs. The CDPC and the HDC are supported by a full-time, bureaucratic office responsible for disaster response preparation. At the time of the Kobe earthquake, this relatively small staff of thirty-six was called the Disaster Management Bureau within the National Land Agency. The bureau was later folded into the Cabinet Office, in January 2001, to bring it closer to the center of decision making.

Despite this overarching national-level organization, as in the United States and most other countries that conduct systematic disaster response planning and training, the Japanese local governments have primary responsibility and authority for managing disasters that occur in their areas of jurisdiction. "Local" in this context exists at two levels: 1) the prefecture level (each with its own elected governor and legislature), and 2) the most local level such as a city or town. Planning and prevention councils similar to those at the national level are replicated at both local levels of government, and emergency response centers – essentially the local equivalent of the HDC – are established when a disaster occurs. As will be discussed below, these headquarters were indeed set up when the Kobe earthquake struck, but the scale of the disaster overwhelmed their ability to communicate and coordinate effectively.

Despite this general level of preparation at the national level and the established bodies and procedures for response at the local level, there was little expectation that an earthquake of this magnitude would strike in the Kobe area. Most seismological predictions focused on the Tokai region (to the east) as the most likely locale for the next big earthquake to hit Japan, and consequently preparations in the Kobe area were not undertaken with the same degree of rigor as elsewhere. Historically, Kobe had been spared major earthquakes, lending a further air of unreality to disaster preparations for this type of event. Generally, if an event is deemed to have a low probability of occurring, it contributes to a lack of seriousness in disaster preparedness efforts. This is true in any country. The United States struggled with this problem at certain points during the Cold War when it attempted to bolster civil defense and preparedness activities. In addition, for man-made crises, it is likely that metropolitan areas such as Tokyo, New York, and Washington take preparation more seriously because they are viewed as more likely victims. The bombing of the Murrah Federal Building in Oklahoma City in the United States and the earthquake in Kobe may have helped to counter this attitude, at least for a while.

The Immediate Response and its Shortfalls

According to most observers and analysts, the response of the Japanese people to the Kobe earthquake was laudable. Individuals in the community did not panic, there was no looting, burglary, or any social disorder, and volunteers readily joined relief activities. For the first month after the disaster approximately twenty thousand individuals a day volunteered to assist in recovery efforts. However, the response by the prefecture and national governments in Japan was far from adequate. One of the shortfalls, in fact, was an inability to integrate this volunteer effort effectively into the larger, government-led response and recovery program.

Beginning at the top of the Japanese government, at least one possibly apocryphal report of the prime minister's morning staff meeting that day had the Kobe earthquake as the fifth agenda item. If true, this placement on the agenda certainly did not reflect the priority of the disaster in the minds of the national-level government once its magnitude was fully understood. Rather, it likely reflected a combination of a lack of understanding of the need for top-level management of the situation and, even more, a lack of understanding in the immediate aftermath of just how serious the incident was. Indeed, information flow out of the region was slow at best. One reason for this was infrastructure damage (electricity and telecommunications) but another reason was the absence of a systematic plan for requesting assistance and a reluctance to ask for specific forms of assistance from the central government. On the latter point, four hours passed before the governor of Hyogo Prefecture asked for help from the Japanese SDF. It then took another five hours for the SDF to respond to the request and a full two days before they arrived in Kobe in any significant numbers.[23] Clearly, communication from the prefecture to national levels of authority needed fixing, and response rates needed to be accelerated. As the crisis evolved, coordination among the central government departments in Tokyo was all but invisible. Then-Prime Minister Tomiichi Murayama largely admitted that bureaucratic missteps and a lack of preparedness significantly undermined recovery efforts. Not surprisingly, the problems with the response effort had a palpable political effect on the sitting government, decreasing its approval rating and increasing its disapproval rating to the highest level since the prime minister took office. In the polling, respondents indicated that the prime reason for their dissatisfaction was the handling of the earthquake.[24]

On the actual response tasks that were required, many fell far short of the mark due to a lack of planning and coordination. The immediate urban search and rescue effort was also deemed totally inadequate, especially considering the number of buildings destroyed, a problem that would have been further compounded had the earthquake occurred during the day when thousands more people would have been trapped in collapsed office buildings and fires. The needs of 250,000 people for emergency food and other basic services were not well met because an effective system of shelter management and supply distribution had not been instituted prior to the earthquake. Access to the scene and transport of relief supplies to the area were hampered because repairs of minor damage were not made to bridges and highways early on, keeping traffic flow reduced for extended periods. Finally, on-scene coordination between response/rescue workers and public safety officials was lacking.[25]

It is important to note that the size, scope, and location of the Kobe earthquake would have taxed even the best-prepared government, but it was clear to both Japanese and outside participants that procedural rigidity and the lack of preparedness exacerbated the situation. Other constraints also hampered response efforts. The lack of large open spaces in the Kobe region made it difficult to concentrate or stage relief resources and personnel. The vast size of the affected area also made communication and assessment – as well as triage – difficult. Given the scope of the disaster, the national-level disaster management bureau that supported the CDPC and the HDC was woefully understaffed, and no mechanism existed at the time to expand it during times of actual crisis. Thirty-six individuals staffing the National Land Agency's Disaster Management Bureau was simply an inadequate number to manage the size and complexity of the necessary coordination efforts.[26]

The poor coordination on the national level and between national and prefecture governments was mirrored on the international front. Like any other assets in a relief or response effort, international organizations, NGOs, and assistance offered bilaterally from other countries can be underutilized and made ineffectual if not coordinated properly with in-country national, state, and local assets. Illustrative of poor planning and bureaucratic snafus following the earthquake, contingents of foreign doctors arrived in Kobe only to be delayed at the airport – in some cases for three days – because they did not have the necessary licenses to practice in Japan. Food, water for drinking and sanitation, blankets, and warm clothing were in short supply for several days after the quake. It took the national government two days to grant permission to have fifty thousand blankets shipped in from the United States, and distribution of emergency supplies stockpiled on U.S. bases in Japan was delayed for several days and then only specific items like tents and plastic sheets were requested by Japanese officials. Of the sixty nations that offered assistance to the Japanese government, offers from only twenty were eventually accepted. The apparent reason for this bureaucratic bungling and ineffective use of international assistance was primarily the fact that no overall strategy, policies, or plans were in place for the coordination of relief efforts (including assistance from international organizations, outside nations, and international NGOs) among national, prefecture, and local authorities, a situation that is only now being addressed and rectified. The problem of limited staff resources to review and process offers of aid was also a frustrating bottleneck.

Preparedness and emergency response are often the most affordable, if not the only possible, mitigation techniques available to many regions for such natural disasters. Indeed, no matter what structural retrofitting may precede an event, it can never entirely prevent the problem, so that a large, prepared emergency response capability will always be required. Clearly in the case of the Kobe earthquake, those preparations were lacking in many areas. After the public outcry over the response of the government, a variety of lessons were identified, and many actions were taken to attempt to change policies and procedures to take those lessons into account.

Lessons

The scope of the disaster was such that it attracted a lot of attention and generated several studies on the response, both in Japan and jointly between Japan and the United States.[27] Lessons drawn by participants in the crisis response effort, by analysts and observers after the fact (both Japanese and American), and by the public and political class were fairly consistent. Overall, most analysts agreed that, despite years of planning and preparation, Japan – at the time of the Kobe earthquake – simply did not possess a reliable crisis management system that could respond to major incidents, regardless of their type.[28] Various aspects of the system came in for criticism and generated suggestions for review and improvement.

The first component of the system that was deemed lacking was at the top of the Japanese government hierarchy, where the command and control capability necessary to manage a crisis of that size simply did not exist. This lack of capability was the result of a number of deficiencies. The first was insufficient centralized knowledge about the capabilities and workings of various ministries and a command and control system ill suited to order and organize them into a timely and coordinated response. Because the HDC was not prepared to manage the plethora of agencies and departments that became involved, each organization tended to execute its own response plan based on its own understanding of the situation. The second shortcoming was an inability to communicate with the field in a systematic and timely manner. Third, the disaster management bureau at the national level was severely understaffed for a crisis of this magnitude. Many of these shortcomings have been addressed by centralizing and strengthening the crisis management functions within the cabinet, as described in chapter 4. Finally, the systems and procedures that were in place at the time of the earthquake had not been practiced sufficiently for this scale of disaster or this type of decision-making pressure, to allow for problems to be worked out before a major crisis occurred. This issue of rehearsal or exercise method emerges in various case studies as a key factor in determining how well a crisis is (or is not) handled. For the most part, Japan gets high marks for the frequency and scale of disaster management exercises, but until recently it rarely tested the command and control functions to the breaking point. In the United States, the opposite tended to be true.

In addition to national-level issues and lessons, analysts identified coordination and cooperation between national and local levels of government as an area that needed improvement in combating and responding to disasters. The shortcomings and subsequent lessons learned at the local level focused on problems similar to those at the national level: lack of knowledge of plans and capabilities of other agencies and levels of government; a limited ability to communicate with higher levels of government; a lack of adequately staffed organizations with responsibility to handle disasters; and a lack of exercises that simulate decision making and test systems to the breaking point.

In the specific area of requesting assistance from the SDF, lessons were learned by both prefecture-level officials and SDF officials. The prefecture officials waited too long to make a formal request for assistance from the SDF, and, when the latter did finally deploy, it did so tentatively and with too little capability. This failure can be traced to a lack of planning, exercising, and coordination, bolstered by a deep wariness about the military still evident in many parts of the Japanese polity. To help solve this problem, Japan's Defense Agency has helped place at least twenty-two former and current SDF officers in local government positions to bolster local civilian crisis management in the future.[29]

Similar to the lack of coordination and planning between the national and local levels of government, officials also recognized that cooperation with and integration of international capabilities as a supplemental part of the response and recovery effort were relatively weak. While not as critical an element as the lack of proper coordination between the national and local levels of government (given the pressing need for an effective response in the first hours or days of a disaster), the failure to acknowledge, accept, and utilize international offers of support further contributed to the Japanese public's perception that the crisis was not being well managed at the national level. In addition, it should be noted that a variety of post-event, lessons-learned efforts have generated, as well, helpful suggestions for improved planning, preparation, and coordination at all levels of Japanese government and in the broader society. These include recommendations for structural changes, procedural innovations, enhanced use of technology, and increased public awareness and participation in preparation, response, and mitigation efforts.

The Tokaimura Nuclear Accident

The Disaster
The worst nuclear power accident in Japan's history took place on September 30, 1999, at the Japan Nuclear Fuel Conversion Company's (JCO) nuclear fuel fabrication plant in Tokaimura, a city approximately ninety miles north of Tokyo. The cause of the accident was operator error, and it occurred when workers at the plant placed too much enriched uranium into a purification tank (approximately seven times the normal amount). The result was a self-sustaining nuclear chain reaction with a release of radioactive materials for close to twenty hours. Three workers inside the room at the time the tank "went critical" received very high doses of radiation – two at levels that proved to be fatal. Heightened radiation levels were also detected not

Partial Map of Japan Showing Area Around Tokaimura

only outside of the room but also outside the facility, up to several kilometers away.

The environmental contamination consequences of the accident were, fortunately, limited in geographic scope and severity, but the health consequences for several workers were severe. One of the three who received the initial high doses of radiation died twelve weeks later and another died seven months later. Twenty-seven more workers were exposed to heightened levels of radiation during operations aimed at gaining control of the accident and stopping the chain reaction.[30] Longer-term health implications for other facility workers and civilians (numbering approximately 670) in the vicinity are still unknown, but are currently not thought to be serious. More serious, in many ways, were the political consequences of the accident, discussed in greater detail below.

The accident was rated a level 4 on the International Nuclear Event Scale, which ranges from zero to 7. On this scale, a zero level event is one that has no significant safety implications, while a 7 would be a major accident with widespread health and environmental consequences. This scale, developed by the International Atomic Energy Agency (IAEA) and the Nuclear Energy Agency of the Organization for Economic Cooperation and Development (OECD), is used as an important communication tool among the members of these bodies. By way of comparison, the Three Mile Island accident (1979) in the United States would have been rated a 5 because of the severe damage onsite even though off-site radioactivity levels were relatively low. Similarly, the Chernobyl accident (1986) in the former Soviet Union, with its large geographical spread of radiation and resulting health effects, was a 7 on the scale.[31]

Japanese Planning and Preparedness

Japan's nuclear power industry is one of the most advanced in the world. It currently ranks third, behind the United States and France, in installed nuclear capacity. The government of Japan's commitment to nuclear power as a key component of fulfilling its energy needs is based largely on its significant dependence on imports of fossil fuels. Currently, nuclear power accounts for about 30 percent of electricity generation in Japan, compared to the 61 percent generated by fossil fuels.[32] Japan is also trying to reduce its carbon dioxide emissions, in part to comply with the Kyoto Protocol agreement on climate change, which provides further incentive for its nuclear program.[33] The fact that all this nuclear power is operating in a densely populated country (336 people per square kilometer, versus 109 in France and 29 in the United States) raises the stakes for Japan's crisis managers. In addition, because it also imports the fuel for the nuclear reactors, Japan endeavors to reduce this dependency by reprocessing spent fuel to recover both uranium and plutonium. It also operates its own uranium enrichment plants so as to be less dependent on other countries for any particular stage of its fuel cycle. Despite growing public opposition to nuclear power (due to the Tokaimura and other less serious incidents), Japan's current ten-year energy plan calls for an expansion of nuclear-powered electricity generation by 30 percent by 2010.

The widespread use of nuclear power plus the possession of all aspects of the nuclear fuel cycle, with the exception of mining uranium, means that Japan has had a long-standing safety and crisis management program for its nuclear facilities. It has, however, also experienced a series of accidents over the years that have, at times, shaken the public's confidence in nuclear power, resulting in a series of reforms to Japan's nuclear safety architecture. Today, the Nuclear and Industrial Safety Agency (Genshiryoku Anzen Hoan-in, or NISA) within the Ministry of Economy, Trade and Industry (METI) is the primary nuclear power regulator in Japan, licensing plants and facilities, and conducting regular safety inspections of all power plants. Closer to the prime minister in the Cabinet Office, policy formulation for nuclear safety and other nuclear energy issues is essentially divided between the Nuclear Safety Commission (Genshiryoku Anzen Iinkai) and the Atomic Energy Commission (Genshiryoku Iinkai), respectively. Much of the day-to-day safety responsibility, however, rests with the electric power companies themselves and with other enterprises associated with the nuclear industry. This was even truer at the time of the Tokaimura accident, a fact that, when combined with the greater fragmentation then

Reorganization of Nuclear Power and Industrial Safety Administrations in Japan

Before the Reorganization of the Central Ministries	After the Reorganization of the Central Ministries in 2001

Agency of Natural Resources and Energy
 	
Safety regulations for:
  nuclear power stations
Safety of:
  electrical power, utility gas, and heat supply
	Nuclear and Industrial Safety Agency (NISA)†
	
	Safety regulations for:
	  refining and processing facilities
	  nuclear power stations (including R&D reactors)
	  fuel reprocessing as well as waste disposal and
	  management facilities
	Safety of:
	  electrical power, utility gas, and heat supply
	  explosives, high-pressure gas, petroleum industrial
	  complexes, LPG, and mines

Environmental Protection and Industrial Location Bureau (Ministry of Industrial Trade and Industry)
 	
Safety of:
  explosives, high pressure gas,
  petroleum industrial complexes, LPG, and mines	

	Ministry of Education, Culture, Sports, Science and Technology
	
	Safety regulations for
	  test and research reactors
	Prevention of:
	  radiation hazards
	Environmental monitoring

Science and Technology Agency
 	
Refining and processing facilities
Test and research reactors
Research and development reactors
Safety regulations for:
  fuel reprocessing as well as waste disposal
  and management facilities
	† NISA functions within METI'S Agency for National Resources and Energy

in bureaucratic oversight, contributed to a disappointing government crisis management performance.

The Immediate Response and its Shortfalls

The accident occurred at 10:35 in the morning. Initial responsibility for both managing the accident and informing other competent authorities rested with JCO corporate officials. Indecision on the part of these officials was apparent when they waited forty-five minutes before notifying national government authorities about the accident.[34] It apparently took another two hours for JCO to ask the local village government for an evacuation order. This order by the village authorities was only then issued at 3:00 p.m. and applied to 200 people living within a 350-meter radius of the plant. The prefecture then issued an advisory to the 313,000 residents living within a 10-kilometer radius of the plant to stay indoors. This advisory did not take place until 10:30 the same evening.

It is interesting that the company was in the middle of the communication chain – first going up to the prefecture-level government and then, separately, down to the village-level authorities. The central government eventually sat above the local operation by means of the specially created Government Accident Countermeasures Headquarters, agreed to at 3:00 p.m. that day and headed by the minister for science and technology. Not until 9:00 p.m. was the Government Task Force for the Accident established and convened, headed by the prime minister. It was clear that the company was not well prepared for a major disaster, particularly in terms of a plan for communicating with both government authorities and the public. JCO did not have a disaster plan, because this particular kind of accident was never anticipated, and it did not establish an authoritative spokesman for the event. The structure for information exchange and command and control among the three main actors (national authorities, local officials, and JCO) was ill defined and poorly tested.

As a result, government agencies at all levels faced several difficulties. After much deliberation, the prefecture level of government declared the event a major disaster, twelve hours after it had occurred. In the meantime, however, rumors circulated and various levels of government gave out conflicting and confusing statements as to what the public in the vicinity should or should not do – ranging from staying inside to not drinking well water to not harvesting crops. The lack of a central spokesperson, either at the company or in the government, allowed poor reporting by the media to spark panic.[35] The national response faced similar shortcomings. The Japanese SDF's chemical warfare defense unit was dispatched by the central government, but the unit was not equipped or trained to handle radiological incidents. This was quickly noted by the media, further undermining the public's confidence in the ability of the government to handle the situation.

On the international front, Japanese officials were busy contacting foreign embassies in Tokyo, including those of the United States and Russia, to see if anyone had experience with this type of accident. The foreign ministry also asked Belgium, Britain, France, Germany, and Sweden for relevant data in requests made through Japanese embassies abroad. Four hours after the government task force convened, it apparently asked USFJ for assistance, but USFJ replied that it was not equipped to handle such accidents. That the Japanese government did not know USFJ's resident capabilities and limitations is perhaps understandable given the uniqueness of the accident, but it demonstrates a lack of communication that could easily be remedied in the future. The United States and Russia formed an impromptu joint response team, in case Japan requested help from outside the country, and the IAEA also made a special response team available to Japan. All of this underscores the ad hoc nature of the international component to this particular crisis response. Japan was interested in outside assistance, but both Japan and the international community were ill prepared to coordinate an appropriate remedy.

In terms of specific responses to the accident itself and mitigation efforts, the JCO had primary responsibility. Approximately sixteen hours after the chain reaction began, JCO officials recognized the need to bring the tank under control and initiate a plan for draining the water in the cooling jacket around the tank. This turned out not to be a simple procedure, requiring dismantling of pipes in areas where workers could only go for very short periods of time because of radiation exposure. This was further evidence of a lack of planning both in the design of the facility and in planning for emergencies of this type. The decision to pump boric acid into the drained cooling jacket as a way of mitigating the chain reaction also had an improvised quality to it, providing further evidence that systematic planning for these kinds of accidents had not taken place at JCO or at any level of government. Even if it was not the government's responsibility to plan for accidents at specific plants, its oversight of accident plans and procedures was clearly insufficient.

Longer-term responses to the accident fell into two categories. The first was identifying those culpable at JCO and bringing criminal charges against them. Approximately one year after the accident and the subsequent investigation, Japanese police arrested six officials from the JCO plant and charged them with professional negligence. In March 2003, sentences were handed down: a fine of one million yen for JCO and suspended sentences for the six employees, punishments that were seen as relatively light considering the seriousness of the accident.[36] The JCO's operating license for the plant was also revoked in early 2000 at the conclusion of the accident investigation by Japanese authorities. While both IAEA and Japanese government reports on the accident placed blame for its occurrence squarely on the workers and managers of the plant, some observers pointed out the dangers of letting this be the only conclusion or even the primary conclusion because it left in place faulty systems at both the company and government level.[37] This charge was partially mitigated when Japan's Nuclear Safety Commission, in its report on the accident, also blamed Japan's Science and Technology Agency (STA) for failure in its oversight functions – essentially not uncovering a series of illegal operational and safety procedures that were in place at the Tokaimura plant. These shortcomings eventually led to the consolidation of nuclear safety oversight at NISA (within METI) as part of the government reorganization in 2001. In addition to its role as regulator, NISA also has its own Nuclear Emergency Preparedness Division to prepare for and help manage accidents, and it currently has senior specialists in emergency preparedness stationed at nineteen off-site centers around the country.

The second, longer-term response involved reforms both in Japan's nuclear industry and in the policies and procedures of the Japanese government, at all levels, for handling future accidents of this type. The accident reinvigorated the debate about the future of nuclear energy in Japan in general and about its safety in particular. At the corporate level, Japan's power companies formed the Nuclear Safety Network, a voluntary association designed to disseminate and improve the safety culture of the entire nuclear industry. This type of voluntary, corporate response is similar to the information sharing and analysis centers being formed in the United States to address cyber security issues. The question of the effectiveness of these types of voluntary efforts versus the economic costs and efficacy of government regulations remains open in each field.

In the wake of the accident, the two competent, national-level authorities for nuclear power – Japan's STA and the Ministry of International Trade and Industry (what became METI in the 2001 government reorganization) agreed on draft legislation to help prevent and, should prevention fail, respond to future nuclear accidents. The draft bills called for periodic government inspections of all nuclear facilities, improved communications capabilities between facilities and government, and enhanced employee training in safety issues. Another draft bill allowed the prime minister to declare a state of emergency and set up a national-level emergency headquarters near accident sites, a role that was previously carried out by local authorities. A final draft bill required nuclear-related facilities, such as the JCO fabrication facility, to conduct the same safety checks as those carried out at nuclear power plants. It would also require employees at these facilities to report illegal practices to government agencies and ministries, not just to internal company watchdogs or safety offices.

The legislation, the Special Measures Law for Nuclear Disasters (Genshiryoku Saigai Taisaku Tokubetsu Sochi Hō), came into force in June 2000, though the basic regulatory and crisis response structure remained until after the 2001 government reorganization, when NISA was launched. By the end of fiscal year 2001, METI established "off-site centers" – essentially crisis management centers – near each nuclear facility in Japan. These centers would be charged with conducting emergency response training and exercises for company employees and local, prefecture, and national government officials. During an actual crisis, the centers, in concert with the national-level Emergency Response Support Center, would act as the local headquarters for responding to the accident (thus forging a tight national-local link). Within the Nuclear Safety Commission in the Cabinet Office, the Radiation Protection and Accident Management Division contributes to preparations and response. The first exercise based on the new legislation took place on October 28, 2000, and involved almost nineteen hundred personnel from eighty-three different organizations and eleven thousand local residents – numbers that themselves point to the difficulties of coordination with any sizable nuclear accident or incident.[38]

While holding exercises is important, it is not sufficient. Lessons must be learned out of exercises and adjustments made. As noted elsewhere in this study, pushing exercise scenarios to the extreme – basically to failure of the response mechanisms – is critical for learning and proper preparation for many of the unknowns that arise in real-life accidents.

Lessons

As with the Kobe earthquake, communication and public relations were critical in Tokaimura, and both JCO and government officials handled them relatively poorly. As with the Kobe earthquake, better analysis and information flow on the criticality of the event was needed to help managers and government officials judge what next steps were needed. Once criticality was assessed, and in the case of Tokaimura, whether the chain reaction was still occurring, swift promulgation of information about the scope of the accident would have helped accident and mitigation units respond more quickly. They also would have reduced the panic in the general public – and the subsequent loss of confidence in both the nuclear power industry and the government. The need to have a national-level policy, operations, and information center for this function was recognized in the aftermath of the crisis, even if local or company officials have the lead in responding to the actual event and its local consequences. The interface on communications and roles and responsibilities among plant officials, local, regional, and national governments needed to be improved.

Overall, what became clear after the Tokaimura accident was that no single entity was ultimately responsible for the entire spectrum of safety issues at Japanese nuclear facilities. This responsibility ranges from prevention through proper design and operation, to response should an accident occur. The companies, nominally responsible, made assumptions that design and established operating procedures would preclude accidents, and so made little to no effort either to prepare for them or to regularly review practices or overall plant designs to ensure that the best safety procedures were being followed. Any lessons learned by companies in this regard were not systematically shared, and in fact information about past accidents tended to be suppressed rather than disseminated to the industry. Government policy and review bodies were not diligent in regularly assessing company plant designs, policies, or practices or whether safety practices were indeed being followed. Later (in 2001), the discovery of cracks on numerous nuclear power plants owned by the Tokyo Electric Power Company, and evidence of concealment of these issues in inspection reports, indicated that both company review and government oversight on safety issues remained incomplete at best.

The deployment of the SDF's chemical weapons defense unit to the accident simply confirmed that Japan did not have a national-level military consequence management response capability for nuclear accidents. The SDF was neither equipped to play this role nor integrated into a national response plan for accidents of this sort. In the future, even if the SDF does not possess the proper units for dealing with nuclear radiation, it could bring other capabilities to bear on a higher-level accident involving radiation, including transportation and communications. In addition, the National Institute of Radiological Sciences (NIRS) is in charge of medical treatment for victims of radiation accidents who cannot be treated by local hospitals, and all three JCO employees overexposed at the facility were taken to NIRS in the city of Chiba after the accident. NIRS only had four beds for contamination victims, so this relatively small accident nearly overwhelmed NIRS' resources in Chiba. The overall lesson is one of being ready to bring the nation's full capabilities to bear in a timely manner in a crisis and consequence management situation.

Nuclear accidents, as evidenced in the 1986 case of Chernobyl, also have the potential to become international issues. Prevailing wind patterns and Japan's geographic location provide some buffer before an accident could affect other countries, but international discussion and cooperation remain an important issue and an opportunity for sharing lessons. The Tokaimura case and Japan's inquiries to a variety of nations clearly showed that the existence of an organization like the IAEA by itself is not a sufficient method of international cooperation. The IAEA is indispensable, but supplementing the IAEA with other bilateral and multilateral cooperative efforts is also important. Perhaps in recognition of this, several weeks after the JCO accident, the U.S. Department of Energy sent experts to Japan to learn more about the event and to consult with JCO and government officials about nuclear safety issues.

In addition, given the presence of U.S. military forces at various locations around Japan, improved coordination with the United States on nuclear accident warning, assessment, and response in and around USFJ base areas is advisable. The Tokaimura accident showed that the Japanese government either did not have, or did not retrieve internally, information regarding the USFJ's capabilities and limitations in this area. USFJ reluctance to share this type of information could also be a problem. At least one report in 2000 indicated that attempts by local officials in Yokosuka, home to the Yokosuka naval base and the home port of the U.S. aircraft carrier *Kitty Hawk,* to discuss response and management issues in case of a nuclear accident at the base were rebuffed by U.S. military representatives as part of a standard policy not to discuss nuclear power. Local officials were planning for a possible contingency involving a U.S. nuclear-powered submarine that began visiting the base in 1997. Channels of communication were eventually opened between the base and local officials on accidents in general, but discussion of the nuclear issue remained off the table.[39]

This particular issue, however, could become more important in 2007 when the conventionally powered *Kitty Hawk* is scheduled to be decommissioned. It is unclear whether the United States will continue to base an aircraft carrier in Japan at that point, and if so, whether it would be the *John F. Kennedy*, the only conventional carrier remaining in the fleet. If Japan is home port to a nuclear-powered carrier, however, the stakes will be raised for cooperation in case of an accident. In this case, instead of working on a plan with local officials for what becomes a public document (as happened in 2000), perhaps U.S. military officials could work with Japanese SDF personnel to plan for certain contingencies more discreetly. In addition, USFJ and the SDF could explore options for the use of U.S. military assets in extreme circumstances, for example, in the area of decontamination or medical facilities. Whatever happens on this front, however, given the sensitivity over nuclear issues related to military forces, enhanced communication and cooperation on nuclear accidents/incidents between USFJ and all levels of the Japanese government are necessary – regardless of the source of the accident.

September 11 Terrorist Attacks in the United States

The Attack

On the morning of September 11, 2001, nineteen members of the Al Qaeda terror network hijacked four airplanes – two out of Logan International Airport in Boston, Massachusetts, one departing from Newark International Airport in New Jersey, and one out of Dulles International Airport near Washington, D.C. The two flights from Boston were deliberately crashed into the two towers of the World Trade Center in New York City approximately forty-five minutes after takeoff. American Airlines flight 77, out of Dulles, crashed into the Pentagon one hour after the first skyscraper in New York was hit. Finally, after passengers attempted to overpower the hijackers on United Airlines flight 93, that plane crashed into an open field in rural Pennsylvania, southeast of Pittsburgh. While the terrorists' intended destination of flight 93 is not certain, its direction and available information indicate that it was also headed for Washington, D.C., with the possible target being the White House, the U.S. Capitol building, or another U.S. government building.

The attacks were devastating, particularly in New York. Close to 3,000 people died in New York, Washington, and Pennsylvania. Those killed in New York included 157 people (passengers and crew) aboard the two airplanes that were crashed into the World Trade Center, office workers and visitors to the buildings, and 370 firefighters, police officers, and other emergency workers who responded to the attacks. Most of those first responders perished when the two towers collapsed from structural damage caused by the impact of the aircraft and the resulting explosion and fires ignited by the jet fuel the planes carried. The number of casualties in the first responder cadre was higher than it would likely have been otherwise due to the timing of the attacks. They occurred during a routine shift change in the fire and police departments, resulting in two shifts of first responders rushing to the scene. It was the largest loss of firefighters in a single incident in American history. Of course, the increased response also likely helped save hundreds of other lives as workers were helped out of the burning and collapsing buildings.

At the Pentagon, 125 people (civilians and military) working at the Defense Department's headquarters were killed, and another 64 passengers from American Airlines flight 77 died in the crash. Because the Pentagon is a low-rise building and set apart from other structures, there were no casualties caused by the later collapse of a part of the building. In Pennsylvania, all 45 passengers and crew on board United Airlines flight 93 died as some of them attempted to wrest control of the airplane from the hijackers. Their efforts saved an unknown number of other lives, depending on the ultimate target of that airplane.

The damage caused by the terrorist attacks went well beyond lives immediately lost. In the first responder community, in addition to the loss of experienced firefighters and policemen, large quantities of equipment were destroyed in the collapse of the World Trade Center towers. Ninety-one New York Fire Department vehicles were destroyed by the collapsing buildings, including eighteen engines, fifteen ladder trucks, and five ambulances. While federal funds were allocated to replace these vehicles, the loss of both the crews and the vehicles reduced New York City's capacity to respond to other crises in the city, which could have been more serious had the attacks been the beginning of a series of strikes against the United States.

In addition, the attacks were not only meant to kill large numbers of people, they were also meant to damage infrastructure and cripple the U.S. economy. While the terrorists did not achieve their objectives of making the United States grind to a halt or accede to their demands because of the damage wrought, both the short-term damage on infrastructure – particularly in the vicinity of the World Trade Center – and on the U.S. and global economies, was significant. In many ways, the damage done to the small area of New York City around the twin towers was analogous to what one might expect in a city such as Tokyo if an earthquake struck, albeit on a smaller geographic scale. Critical infrastructures – electricity, water, gas, transportation, and telecommunications – were all damaged to varying degrees in the attacks. This disruption of services affected how easily emergency crews could respond and contributed to the longer-term economic damage to the city and the region.

In particular, the outages of electricity and telecommunications made response significantly more difficult. On the electrical grid, five of seven electrical feeder cables in the area were destroyed, two substations adjacent to one of the smaller buildings in the World Trade Center complex were destroyed when it collapsed, and one electrical substation near the South Street Seaport was damaged and lost service. Fortunately, the local network structure of New York City's electrical grid limited cascading effects and allowed power to be restored relatively quickly. If the electrical grid had been more centralized, as it is in some other major U.S. cities, the damage would have cascaded, creating wider-spread problems.

The attacks in New York affected telecommunications in two ways. In addition to the electrical power outage that cut some communications capabilities, the increased demand for both landline and cell phone circuits overwhelmed the systems' capacities. By chance, the attacks also severely damaged a major telecommunications company's central switching network, which was located at a building next to the World Trade Center complex. Collapsing girders damaged the building in which a major call center was housed, and falling debris cut through the street to sever fiber optic cable bundles running under the street. Finally, repeaters for the emergency call system in the city – the 911 system – were located on the twin towers and were knocked out when the buildings were damaged and collapsed. While this did not slow the overall response, many calls from victims in the towers – with possibly useful information on location and damage – went unanswered for hours until, tragically, it was too late.

Transportation networks were also damaged and otherwise affected by the attacks on September 11. The Port Authority Trans-Hudson commuter rail station, located directly under the twin towers, handled sixty-six thousand passengers daily before the attacks. While a temporary station has been erected, rebuilding this central terminal for commuters into New York City awaits the rebuilding of the entire World Trade Center site. On a broader scale, the attacks led to the grounding of all airplanes over or approaching U.S. airspace on the day of the attacks. Full-scale air travel in the United States was not restored for close to a week, with some major airports, such as Logan in Boston and Reagan National in Washington, D.C., remaining closed for significantly longer periods. The airline industry as a whole, already suffering a $3 billion shortfall in the summer of 2001 from a general economic decline, suffered even greater losses (estimated at $10 billion just in the last four months of 2001) as the public declined to return to the skies in pre-September 11 numbers. The negative impact on the airline industry, and associated travel industries, in the United States continued with several major airlines filing for, and receiving, bankruptcy protection against their creditors.

U.S. Planning and Preparedness

An examination of U.S. planning and preparedness for an attack of the type that took place on September 11 can be broken down into two categories. The first category is the national-level planning and preparedness to detect, deter, and if possible prevent catastrophic terrorist attacks on the United States and on its interests overseas. The second is the national, state, and local-level planning and preparedness to respond to attacks, should they occur, and to manage and mitigate the consequences of those attacks, including those that could use WMD. The two tracks are intertwined in that preparation to respond to attacks presupposes a realization that such attacks are not just possible but indeed probable. As the Japanese government did in the cases of the Kobe earthquake and the Tokaimura nuclear plant accident, in the aftermath of large-scale domestic and overseas incidents, the U.S. government responded both to enhance prevention and detection efforts and to enhance response and mitigation policies and procedures. The follow-up to these efforts and their scope, however, tended to fade over time as the belief that attacks would recur, or indeed escalate, diminished or as other imperatives took precedence.

The threat of terrorism to the United States was recognized during the Cold War period, but at that point it was put in the context of nation-state-sponsored acts usually associated with the ongoing struggle between the West and the East. The Clinton administration formally recognized the more amorphous threat of international terrorism to the United States and its interests, as one of a list of problems labeled "transnational phenomena," in its 1994 national security strategy document.[40] The concern about catastrophic terrorist attacks, both within the United States and overseas, received an unfortunate boost with the sarin poison gas attacks, perpetrated by the Aum Shinrikyo cult on March 19, 1995, against the Tokyo subway and with the domestic terrorist bombing of the Murrah Federal Building in Oklahoma City on April 19, 1995. Terrorist attacks on U.S. interests overseas also received heightened attention when a U.S. military assistance mission in Saudi Arabia was bombed, with the loss of five Americans and two Indians in November 1995, and subsequently when a truck bomb was detonated at the Khobar Towers U.S. Air Force housing complex in Dhahran, Saudi Arabia, in June 1996, causing nineteen deaths and hundreds of injuries.

The sarin gas attack in Tokyo enhanced U.S. interest in the possibility that terrorist groups might obtain and use WMD in their attacks. The threat of what came to be called "loose nukes" – nuclear weapons that might find their way from less secure weapons development and storage facilities in the states of the former Soviet Union – was increasingly linked not just to rogue states seeking such a capability but also to terrorist groups that might seek these weapons as well. Prevention efforts in this area were largely confined to a congressional initiative begun in 1991 – dubbed the Nunn-Lugar program after the authorizing legislation's co-sponsors – designed to strengthen the safety and security of nuclear weapons-associated material and know-how, and other WMD material in the states of the former Soviet Union. Efforts in the first Clinton administration were also made to enhance the ability of customs officials and other border security forces in the former Soviet Union and Eastern and Central Europe to detect the smuggling of radioactive materials across borders.

Two other major attacks on U.S. interests overseas, the first in August 1998, against the U.S. embassies in Nairobi, Kenya, and Dar es Salaam, Tanzania, and the second in October 2000, against the destroyer USS *Cole* as it refueled at a harbor in Yemen, both prompted greater scrutiny of Islamist terrorist groups, specifically Al Qaeda. The attacks also led to a variety of studies and resulting changes in policies and practices designed to enhance the protection of U.S. embassies and U.S. military forces deployed overseas. They also sparked further studies and reviews, endorsed by both the administration and Congress, on the threat of terrorist use of WMD.[41] Some of the recommendations of these various committees, particularly those of the accountability review boards for the embassy bombings, repeated recommendations for improving embassy security that had been made by previous panels and commissions of experts, but tragically many were not funded or carried out.[42]

Studies and inquiries in the wake of the September 11 attacks indicated that some information existed within the U.S. government that was relevant to the attacks. A joint congressional inquiry, however, concluded that this information did not identify the time, place, and/or specific nature of the attacks. The general belief of the U.S. intelligence community after the attacks on the U.S. embassies in East Africa was that future attacks would most likely take place against U.S. interests overseas, even though information existed indicating that direct attacks on the United States proper were being planned.[43] Prior to the September 11 attacks, some individuals within the law enforcement and intelligence communities were of the opinion that Osama bin Laden and Al Qaeda were greater threats to the United States than was generally acknowledged or agreed upon in the general interagency community.[44] Still others possessed pieces of information or sought to take actions that could have at least revealed more of the plans for September 11, but were unable to make their voices heard at a national level. Whether this failure to take up the views of these individuals or to merge the information held by various elements of the U.S. government together was a catastrophic failure is still open to debate. As noted obliquely in the congressional inquiry, it is not clear – even if all information had been pulled together and the voices of the "alarmists" heeded – that the attacks could have been either deterred or prevented. Certainly, there is an understanding that the system could have worked much better; the bureaucratic responses to this determination are detailed in the next chapter.

The two 1995 attacks, one in the United States and the other in Tokyo, prompted the Clinton administration to develop a more comprehensive policy on crisis response and consequence management in the case of future terrorist attacks, including those using WMD. This policy, issued by the White House as PDD 39 on June 21, 1995, gave unprecedented attention to the issue of WMD in the hands of terrorists and began in a more systematic manner to define the roles and responsibility of various U.S. government agencies in both preventing and responding to future attacks. This policy was updated in May 1998, just three months before the Al Qaeda attacks on the U.S. embassies in Kenya and Tanzania, with PDD 62, which established the Office of the National Coordinator for Security, Infrastructure Protection, and Counter-Terrorism, an organization that was essentially an enhanced directorate within the National Security Council staff system. The increased staff and prestige were supposed to enable the national coordinator to improve cooperation amongst various U.S. agencies. The office also was given, after long battles with both the agencies involved and the Office of Management and Budget, the right to "provide advice regarding budgets for counter-terrorism programs." The decision directive also provided this newly established office with the interagency lead in developing guidelines that might be needed for crisis management – in other words for responding to a major terrorist attack and managing its consequences.

Lessons

In sum, the United States was fairly well prepared for September 11 in the abstract, but interagency exchange and analysis of information proved to be inadequate. New York City and Washington handled the consequence management side of things about as well as could be expected, though the situation did overwhelm certain communications and management functions in New York. Also, authorities there failed to seriously consider the potential that one or both of the towers could collapse as quickly as they did (within about an hour and a half of impact), with tragic consequences. In terms of prevention, international terrorism had been recognized as a growing phenomenon in the mid-1990s, and organizational and policy changes, at least at the center of the U.S. interagency (the White House and National Security Council staff), had been made to enhance U.S. ability to detect, deter, and respond to catastrophic terrorist attacks, including those using weapons of mass destruction. Al Qaeda had been recognized as a major threat to U.S. interests because of its attacks on the two U.S. embassies in East Africa and on the USS *Cole* in Yemen. Indeed, in the summer of 2001, the U.S. interagency – led by the national coordinator – had been put on high alert over a possible attack by Al Qaeda.

After weeks of waiting and after no further intelligence information was forthcoming about the timing, type, or scope of a potential attack, the extra precautions were eased – just weeks before the actual attacks.

As with the Kobe earthquake, the literal, political, and psychological impacts on the country were profound, and the lessons learned from the crisis are still being developed at a variety of political levels and in the private sector. Focusing on the national political level, lessons were learned both on the deterrence/prevention side and on the crisis/consequence management side. Much of the public debate in the aftermath of the attacks focused on the questions of why the U.S. government did not know the attacks were imminent and why it failed to prevent them. Just as importantly, though, questions of how the crisis was managed as it was unfolding and how the consequences were handled in the days, weeks, and months that followed were examined and remedies were adopted. In fact, the organizational and policy changes designed to fix, in particular, shortcomings in detection and prevention within the U.S. government also have affected how the United States will respond in managing future crises of this kind and in mitigating their consequences. Whether this has resulted in improvements in the crisis and consequence management of future attacks of this sort remains to be seen.

The lessons drawn from September 11 about the ability of the U.S. government to detect, prevent, deter, and respond directly to terrorist attacks on the United States and overseas were outlined most fully in the U.S. Congress's joint intelligence committee inquiry into the attacks. The findings of this investigation focused on two sets of shortcomings. The first was the inability of the U.S. intelligence community to obtain, aggregate, and correctly analyze the information that it had at its disposal regarding the September 11 attacks and on the issue of global terrorist threats against the United States more generally. The inquiry concluded that both the Central Intelligence Agency and the Federal Bureau of Investigation failed to identify and aggressively monitor the activities of suspected or known terrorists both within the United States and abroad.

Select Recommendations from the Congressional Joint Inquiry

- Congress should amend the National Security Act of 1947 to create and sufficiently staff a statutory Director of National Intelligence (a Cabinet level position) who shall be the President's principal advisor on intelligence.

- The National Security Council [in conjunction with other relevant offices] should prepare, for the President's approval, a U.S. government-wide strategy for combating terrorism, both at home and abroad, including the growing terrorism threat posed by the proliferation of WMD and associated technologies. This strategy should identify and fully engage those foreign policy, economic, military, intelligence, and law enforcement elements that are critical to a comprehensive blueprint for success in the war against terrorism.

- The State Department, in consultation with the Department of Justice, should review and report to the President and the Congress by June 30, 2003, on the extent to which revisions in bilateral and multilateral agreements, including extradition and mutual assistance treaties, would strengthen U.S. counterterrorism efforts.

- The President should review and consider amendments to the Executive Orders, policies and procedures that govern the national security classification of intelligence information, in an effort to expand access to relevant information for federal agencies outside the Intelligence Community, for state and local authorities, which are critical to the fight against terrorism, and for the American public.

When information was available about the activities of suspected terrorists or terrorist groups, it was not shared and aggregated in a manner that would have proved useful to policy makers charged with taking preventive measures.

The second set of findings focused on a lack of appreciation, within both the intelligence community and the policy community, of the scope and severity of the threat posed to the United States by Al Qaeda and a consequent lack of an effective counterterrorism strategy for combating that organization. The inquiry noted that the response to previous terrorist attacks, and to terrorism in general, had a law enforcement emphasis, again reflecting the relative threat level that this issue was accorded. This is not just a procedural or organizational indictment but a policy one as well. It relates to the broader question of the appropriate focus for U.S. national security policy in the post-Cold War era, and the issue spans two administrations. More specific shortcomings in preventing this particular set of attacks, such as the failure in airport security procedures (e.g., inadequate passenger screening and weak cockpit doors), were also identified in separate lessons-learned exercises within the U.S. government.

On the crisis response and consequence management side of the equation, performance was generally not found to be as lacking. In part this was because the terrorists chose to attack the two U.S. metropolitan areas most able to respond to large-scale crises. In part, also, criticism of response efforts – particularly those of first responders – was muted at the outset because of the large number who perished in attempts to rescue victims from the twin towers. The primary lessons that were eventually aired focused on the adequate funding and training for first responders, particularly in incidents that could involve WMD. Information flow and communication, as in the Kobe earthquake in Japan, could have been better – particularly between the local and national levels – but in the case of September 11, the destruction was not so widespread as to inhibit prompt communication from the scene. The response was so massive in the case of September 11, both on the part of the government and the public, that one problem was coordinating efforts – particularly between the formal and informal systems that were set up to handle the aftermath of the attacks. On the whole, however, most of these issues were dealt with at the local level, and the sheer intensity and volume of the response overcame coordination issues. That said, if the attacks had continued, or if they had been coordinated with attacks of other sorts – such as on the communications or electrical grid on a nation-wide basis – the response and recovery efforts could have been severely hampered. The fact that the terrorist attacks resulted in destruction much more extensive than imagined in contingency scenarios has made crisis and consequence management planners work to ensure that even larger-scale attacks in multiple locations could be handled at both the local and national levels.[45]

Much work remains to be done with regard to adequately funding, equipping, and training first responders around the country for the new tasks they are being required to perform. Two reports by the Council on Foreign Relations highlighted various shortcomings in this area, including a lack of access to potentially valuable intelligence information for police forces at the local level, short-term (instead of longer-term) federal funding commitments that make local communities reluctant to spend the necessary matching investments for improving response capabilities (especially for equipment to deal with NBC attacks), and a general lack of federal funding for equipment and training for first responders and for upgrades to critical infrastructure. These task force reports made a number of specific organizational recommendations, including the establishment of a National Institute for Emergency Preparedness within DHS to work with state and local governments on sharing best practices, the transformation of the House Select Committee on Homeland Security into a standing committee to help streamline the federal budgetary process, and other improvements aimed at better serving the needs of first responders.[46] These task force reports are certainly not the final word on the issue, but there is general agreement that more can be done by the national government to support local first responders as they struggle with tight local budgets and new burdens.

Cyber Security and Critical Infrastructure Protection

The Threat

Concern about the security of U.S. and Japanese critical infrastructures, including particularly the cyber elements that support and enhance them, grew throughout the 1990s.[47] In both the United States and Japan, the combination of technological advances, particularly with respect to cyber communications and the increasingly regular use of the Internet for government and business, together with the search for new national security paradigms after the end of the Cold War, led to an increased awareness of the importance of critical infrastructures and of their vulnerability to attacks by individuals, non-state actors, or states.

In one of the earliest national-level attempts to assess the vulnerabilities of critical infrastructures and begin to design policy responses to these vulnerabilities, President Clinton issued an executive order in July 1996 establishing the President's Commission on Critical Infrastructure Protection. In October 1997, the commission published a report with three major conclusions. The first was that the United States was becoming increasingly reliant on its critical infrastructures, particularly information and communications systems, for its safety and well-being. Second, and in light of this growing dependency, it was becoming easier for certain individuals and groups to inflict damage on these information network systems. Finally, because of this combination of increasing dependence and vulnerability, the commission recommended that the government focus on information assurance and begin a public-private partnership to improve the protection of these vital systems in the years to come.[48]

Similarly, Tokyo's concern for cyber security grew out of its efforts in 1997 to advance Japan's use of information and telecommunications as part of a broader plan for structural economic reform. The initiative, part of then-Prime Minister Hashimoto's emphasis on electronic commerce and the use of the Internet in delivering government services, had some early elements that focused on cyber security. The initiatives, directed from the Prime Minister's Advanced Information and Telecommunication Society Promotion Headquarters, were carried out primarily by two ministries, the Ministry of Posts and Telecommunications (MPT) and the ministry that later became METI. They included support for a national virus control center – an early form of a computer emergency response team (CERT) – and for technological research and development aimed at improving encryption and authentication capabilities.

A combination of the year 2000 (Y2K) computer issue and the rise of numerous computer viruses and hacks of government websites in both the United States and Japan further increased awareness of, and concern for, computer network security in the late 1990s and early part of the twenty-first century.[49] In 1998, the United States received a wakeup call to the national security dimensions of the cyberspace threat. The incident, eventually called Solar Sunrise, had U.S. military systems under electronic assault, with someone on a computer in the United Arab Emirates the apparent source. The targets of the attack were unclassified logistics, administrative, and accounting systems essential to the management and deployment of military forces. They were being penetrated at the same moment that the United States was contemplating a military action against Iraq in response to its failure to comply with UN inspection teams trying to uncover evidence of its WMD programs. The timing of the attacks raised suspicions that this was the first wave of a major cyber attack by a hostile nation. It turned out later that two teenagers from California, under the direction of a sophisticated Israeli hacker, himself a teenager, had orchestrated the attacks using hacker tools readily available on the Internet. They had attempted to hide their involvement by connection through overseas computers. The incident pointed out the difficulty of knowing whether attacks are being perpetrated by individuals, criminal or terrorist groups, or other states.

In early February 2000, computer servers hosting several of the largest commercial websites on the Internet were flooded with connection requests, clogging systems. These so-called distributed denial-of-service (DDOS) attacks paralyzed the Internet. Through close cooperation between U.S. and Canadian law enforcement investigators, it was discovered that a Canadian teenager had been breaking into computers around the world for months. He retained control over these compromised servers, creating a "zombie army" that on command would flood the servers of his next corporate victim. It is estimated that the slowdowns and outages that occurred resulted in more than $1 billion in economic losses.

A series of viruses and worms has also caused significant economic damage around the world since 2000. One, the I Love You virus, began infecting computers around the globe in May 2000. First detected in Asia, the virus swept quickly around the world in a wave of indiscriminate attacks on both government and private-sector networks. By the time the destructive pace of the virus had been slowed, it had infected nearly sixty million computers and caused an estimated $13 billion in damage. This virus, written and sent out by a computer science dropout in the Philippines, was the first in a series of global threats to the Internet that have become more virulent and dangerous. The next global virus, Code Red, infected 150,000 computer systems in fourteen hours, but the damage it caused was less widespread than anticipated because of effective communication and action by computer administrators. In fall 2001 a new type of threat, a combination of virus and Internet worm called NIMDA, spread across the globe even more rapidly than Code Red. While it did not cause the damage of the previous virus thanks to better security measures, it showed that hackers were becoming more sophisticated in how to spread their attacks. In January 2003, another Internet worm, SQL Slammer, proliferated around the world at an unprecedented rate – infecting 90 percent of all vulnerable servers worldwide in approximately ten minutes. The worm damaged banking networks, snarled government computers worldwide, and slowed many corporate systems to the point where they were inaccessible. The speed with which SQL Slammer spread presented a new threat to computer security systems, demonstrating that keeping up with security software patches or downloading such protection after an attack of this type would not be sufficient. After examining this latest spate of attacks, some computer security experts have expressed the opinion that in the battle between virus writers and antivirus software, the virus writers appear to be winning.

In addition to these global events, Japan became much more aware of the computer security threat after a series of hacker attacks aimed at the Japanese government in January 2000. These attacks, linked in part to a controversial forum in Osaka regarding the 1937 Nanjing Massacre, defaced government websites and destroyed data on some government computer networks.[50] While the damage itself was not substantial and the attacks were stopped relatively easily by disconnecting the computer sites from the Internet, they also pointed out how easily Japanese government websites could be penetrated. Most of the attacks were perpetrated using hacking tools available on the Internet. In April 2001, another spate of hacker attacks targeted Japanese government websites and computer networks belonging to the Liberal Democratic Party (LDP) and a major publishing house. This series of incidents was in response to the publishing of a new history textbook that some believed downplayed Japanese atrocities in China and Korea during World War II. Both sets of incidents appear to have been what is known as "patriotic hacking" – a relatively uncoordinated set of attacks by students and other activists overseas, at times with the complicity of a foreign government.

Outside of patriotic hacking, many of the virus and worm attacks over the past five years appear to be the work of individuals without a political agenda. However, the potential for attacks and damage by terrorist groups and even states, each of which has political objectives, remains significant. From Al Qaeda computers recovered by U.S. intelligence in Afghanistan, it is now clear that elements of that terrorist organization were at least investigating methodologies for cyber attacks and were looking at possible targets for such attacks in the United States. Al Qaeda operatives visited hacker sites on the Internet and downloaded tools and strategies for breaking into computer networks. They also conducted surveillance of computer networks that help to run electrical power, water, transportation, and communications grids in the United States. Military officials in the southern Republic of Korea (ROK) are concerned that North Korea is enhancing its computer hacking capabilities in advance of a possible crisis on the peninsula.[51] While such capabilities may be focused primarily on the heavily networked ROK, they could easily be aimed at the United States and/or Japan in a future crisis.

U.S. and Japanese Planning and Preparedness

In the United States, the October 1997 report by the president's commission provided the impetus for both policy and bureaucratic change on how cyber security was approached. Just over six months later, the Clinton administration issued PDD 63, the main policy directive on critical infrastructure protection. Based on the assumption central to the report by the president's commission, that the critical infrastructures and cyber-based information systems of the United States were increasingly vulnerable, the directive listed a primary goal and timeframe for this issue area:

> No later than the year 2000, ... the United States shall have achieved and shall maintain the ability to protect our nation's critical infrastructures from intentional acts that would significantly diminish the abilities of ... [the federal government to perform national security tasks, state and local governments to maintain order and deliver minimal services, and the private sector to ensure functioning of the economy].[52]

The policy document directed the creation of a public-private partnership to reduce vulnerability, designating different federal agencies as lead liaisons with their respective private sector counterparts. The private sector was also asked, working with the government lead agency, to designate a private sector coordinator to represent that industry area. Together, these groups were to develop sector-based national infrastructure assurance plans. At a higher policy level, the president created the National Infrastructure Assurance Council, consisting of private sector representatives, federal lead agencies, and state and local government officials, and chaired by a national coordinator who was dual-hatted as a senior member of the National Security Council staff. An entity within the Department of Commerce, the Critical Infrastructure Assurance Office (CIAO), was created to coordinate all of the various sector liaisons and communicate regularly with the private sector.

In addition to these public-private coordination mechanisms, two types of centers for information sharing and analysis were established by the decision directive. The first was an expansion of an existing warning and analysis center at the FBI into the full-scale National Infrastructure Protection Center (NIPC), a law enforcement entity charged with assessing and warning on vulnerability issues and serving as the law enforcement investigation and response entity for threats to or attacks on critical infrastructure. The second were sector-based information sharing and analysis centers (ISACs) for the private sector entities. ISACs were intended to have a technology focus and were not intended to address either regulatory or law-enforcement missions.

The overall approach was based on the premise that government should, in areas other than the government's own critical infrastructures, act as a coordinator and facilitator rather than as a regulator for the private sector. Minimal reorganization of the federal government was undertaken, with a senior-level coordinator instead being appointed and with existing federal agencies being given new mandates to address this burgeoning issue area. A large part of the initial effort was focused on getting both private industry and the public in general to understand the issue – that critical infrastructures existed, were becoming more vulnerable, and were increasingly tied to and dependent upon cyber infrastructures. The next step was to develop the connections, trust, and mechanisms to allow rapid sharing of information on vulnerabilities, attacks, and remedies between the government and the private sector. Even in the initial analysis, it was recognized that international outreach and cooperation would be necessary, but that aspect of policy development was put on a slower track during the Clinton administration and the early days of the Bush administration until national policies, procedures, and protocols were established.

Planning and preparedness for attacks on critical infrastructures and particularly attacks on cyber networks in Japan slightly lagged behind similar efforts by the United States. Through 1999, each ministry or agency within the Japanese government was responsible for its own network security measures. In late 1999, the Cabinet Secretariat began convening meetings of relevant directors general to discuss IT security. The result was an action plan, issued in January 2000, for protecting government information systems against threats from cyberspace. As was noted above, the intense spate of hacker attacks on Japanese government websites took place just weeks later, providing impetus for speedy implementation of the plan and a deeper review of both the threat and the various measures being taken by the government and the Japanese private sector to combat it. In the aftermath of the January 2000 attacks, a branch for IT security was also established at the

Cabinet Secretariat for National Security and Crisis Management – a similar step to that briefly taken in the United States of appointing a national coordinator with established authority – to report directly to the head of government rather than to an individual cabinet ministry or agency. This branch chaired interagency meetings, resulting in a Cabinet Office plan, issued in July 2000, called Guidelines for IT Security.

These guidelines also led to an enhanced focus on security issues in a new January 2001 law, the Basic Law on the Formation of an Advanced Information and Telecommunications Network Society. An outgrowth of the earlier focus by the Japanese government on bolstering Japan's advantages in information technology, the law contained a far more prominent place for security issues than had been the case when the issue of IT first was discussed in Japan. The basic law, and the plans flowing from it, also included significant provisions for engaging the private sector more vigorously on security issues. On the more traditional national security and law enforcement sides, the basic law and its implementation also led to the creation of new centers in the NPA. The NPA created the dedicated Cyber-Police Force in 2001 to combat cyber terrorism at the agency headquarters with supporting analytical units at each of the seven NPA regional bureaus. In addition, the government of Japan recognized the need for greater international cooperation on these issues, indicating that it would work to strengthen bilateral ties and work through international organizations such as the OECD and the G-8 to address critical infrastructure and cyber security issues.

Shortfalls and Lessons

Unlike the other individual cases discussed in this study, the task of identifying shortfalls and lessons for the United States and Japan in the case of cyber security issues is less clear. No single catastrophic event in this area has occurred since each government and society has begun to organize for the threat, but several smaller-scale events have provided insights into problems endemic to the protection of critical infrastructures and ensuring cyber security.

Despite the recognition in both the United States and Japan that private industry owns and operates the vast majority of critical infrastructures and that communication between government and industry on cyber security is critical, an October 2002 incident illustrated that the system in place in each country is far from perfect. In what at the time was termed the largest and most sophisticated attack on the Internet, DDOS assaults were launched at the thirteen "root servers" that provide the primary roadmap for almost all Internet communications. While the attacks did not result in any noticeable slowing of the Internet, the size and scope of the attempt were novel. In addition, despite the fact that the owners/controllers of the root server networks were almost immediately aware of the attacks and took steps to mitigate the situation, no one thought to notify the U.S. federal government of the incident until nearly twelve hours after it occurred.[53]

Communication between the private and public sectors on computer security overall is inadequate for a variety of reasons. A survey conducted in 2002 by the Computer Security Institute and the San Francisco FBI revealed that only about 36 percent of private firms that experienced a computer intrusion reported it to law enforcement. Some apparently feared negative publicity, others thought that competitors could use the information to their advantage, and still others simply did not know whom to contact.[54] Given the pace at which Internet attacks and incidents occur and spread, the lack of a fail-safe communication mechanism, or indeed even the habit of sharing information, is troubling and points to an area of response that could be greatly improved.

While communication between public and private sector entities concerned with cyber security is still less than perfect on a national level, the addition of the international dimension complicates the issue immensely. In the case of the I Love You virus, U.S. and Philippine law enforcement authorities cooperated well and eventually apprehended the computer-school dropout who wrote and propagated the virus. The problem, however, was that Philippine authorities discovered there were no laws on the books in their country to hold or prosecute the man in question. Writing and distributing highly damaging code over the Internet was not, at the time, a criminal offense in the Philippines. This issue has been recognized in many countries, and significant efforts have been made to ensure that certain cyber activities are criminalized and that laws across countries are harmonized. One major effort that has come to fruition is the Council of Europe's Convention on Cybercrime, signed by member states and others who collaborated in its drafting (including the United States and Japan) in November 2001. Once the treaty enters into force, with five ratifications, it will likely be open to accession by non-drafters. In the meantime, Washington is encouraging non-signatories to ensure that their laws on cyber crime are at least consistent with the provisions of the treaty. Even if laws are harmonized, rapid communications and procedures for law enforcement cooperation on these types of issues will have to be more fully fleshed out to address the potential threats adequately.

Japan has learned similar lessons, with many of the major hack attacks on its government systems being traced to overseas points of origin, particularly China and the ROK. Like the United States, Japan began its programs on cyber security as a national effort and slowly added the international dimension. It has concentrated its efforts in multilateral forums, working with the Council of Europe on drafting the cyber crime convention and working – primarily with Australia – within the realms of APEC and the Association of Southeast Asian Nations (ASEAN) to enhance the capabilities of less highly developed countries in the Pacific to take steps to improve their own cyber security efforts.

On a bilateral level, the United States and Japan have made some progress harmonizing priorities and establishing methods of communication (discussed in chapter 4), but more can be done. Given limited budgets and staffing resources, it is understandable that additional bilateral consultations on these issues might be labeled a lower priority, but one could also argue that it is precisely during this nascent stage when cooperation will (or will not) more firmly establish patterns and mechanisms for collaboration that will pay dividends in the future. Finally,

Japan has focused its critical infrastructure protection efforts initially on government systems, with the breadth and depth of the public-private partnership not being as well developed as it might be hoped. This is in part due to bureaucratic caution by the Japanese government, but it is also because Japanese industry is unwilling to engage seriously on an issue that it sees as requiring an extra expenditure of resources, which can be difficult to justify in a continuing weak economy.

Notes for Chapter Three

19 Kansai Council (Economic and Social Research Institute, Cabinet Office, Economic Research Institute 2002 version).

20 Tsuneo Katayama, "Lessons From the 1995 Great Hanshin Earthquake of Japan" (Institute of Industrial Science, University of Tokyo, 1996).

21 Information about the earthquake's impact from Hyogo Prefecture and City of Kobe.

22 The $90 billion expenditure broke down as follows: reconstruction of infrastructure, approximately 65 percent; housing and welfare, approximately 18 percent; and industrial promotion, approximately 17 percent. Thirty-eight percent of the expenditure subsidized was national expenditure, 43 percent was socialized local expenditure, and 19 percent was unsubsidized local expenditures. Approximately 70 percent of the total amount was financed by public debt. OSIPP-IFPA workshop presentation, November 29, 2000.

23 OSIPP-IFPA workshop presentation, November 29, 2000.

24 *Asahi Shimbun* telephone poll conducted January 27 and 28, 1995. *Yomiuri Shimbun* and *Nihon Keizai Shimbun* polls yielded similar results at the time.

25 *Comprehensive Study of the Great Hanshin Earthquake*, UNCRD Research Report Series, no. 12 (Nagoya, Japan: United Nations Centre for Regional Development, 1995).

26 The National Land Agency's Disaster Management Bureau was the full-time, bureaucratic office responsible for coordinating disaster response (in support of the CDPC and HDC). In January 2001, Japanese government reorganization transferred the Disaster Management Bureau from the National Land Agency to the Cabinet Office, and increased its staff from thirty-six to fifty (roughly its size today). It is led by a minister of state for disaster management, national emergency legislation (*bōsai-yūji hōsei tantō daijin*).

27 United States-Japan earthquake policy symposia and high-level earthquake policy cooperation forums documents available at FEMA, *Mitigation: Reducing Risk Through Mitigation*, http://www.app1.fema.gov/mit/usjapan.htm. Numerous other studies were conducted.

28 Editorial in *Japan Times* (January 26, 1995) quoted in Kathleen J. Tierney and James D. Goltz, "Emergency Response: Lessons Learned from the Kobe Earthquake," a preliminary paper from the University of Delaware's Disaster Research Center, April 3, 2000, http://www.udel.edu/DRC/preliminary/260.pdf. Several other reports came to similar conclusions.

29 *Japan Times*, "SDF Officers Take Local Government Positions," June 6, 2003.

30 A detailed technical report on the accident is available from the International Atomic Energy Agency, "Report on the Preliminary Fact Finding Mission Following the Accident at the Nuclear Fuel Processing Facility in Tokaimura, Japan," 1999 (hereafter IAEA Tokaimura Report).

31 The full scale, with explanatory notes and examples, is available at *IAEA.org*, http://www.iaea.org/Publications/Factsheets/English/ines-e.pdf.

32 Japan's Ministry of Economy, Trade and Industry, *Statistical Handbook of Japan 2003*.

33 Officially, the Kyoto Protocol to the United Nations Framework Convention on Climate Change.

34 Japan's Science and Technology Agency (STA) had oversight responsibility for the facility and was contacted around 11:19 a.m. Local government officials in Tokaimura were notified by JCO at around 11:34 a.m. From the IAEA Tokaimura Report.

35 One news organization accidentally took pictures of a building near the JCO that was damaged in a fire two years earlier and published the pictures briefly on the Internet, frightening Japanese who saw the photos and leading other news organizations to report as late as early the next morning that an explosion probably occurred at the site, which may have blown off the roof of the facility (National Public Radio in the United States aired one such report at 5:30 a.m., October 1, 1999).

36 Bayan Rahman, "Japanese Nuclear Group 'Negligent,'" *Financial Times*, March 4, 2003.

37 Najmedin Meshkati and Joseph Deato, "Japan Must Commence Nuclear Reforms," *Japan Times*, October 2, 2000.

38 Nuclear Power Engineering Corporation, *2001 Annual Report*, 46. This corporation contributed to the exercise.

39 Steve Liewer and Mayumi Yamamoto, "Yokosuka City Draws Up Plan for Dealing with Nuclear Accident," *Stars and Stripes*, July 27, 2000.

40 The White House, *A National Security Strategy of Engagement and Enlargement* (Washington, D.C., July 1994).

41 For the executive summaries of the various commission reports, see U.S. Senate, *Strategies for Homeland Defense, A Compilation by the Committee on Foreign Relations, United States Senate*, September 26, 2001, http://www.access.gpo.gov/congress/senate.

42 U.S. Department of State, *Report of the Secretary of State's Advisory Panel on Overseas Security* (Washington, D.C., July 1995).

43 *Joint Inquiry into Intelligence Community Activities Before and After the Terrorist Attacks of September 11, 2001*, report of the U.S. Senate Select Committee on Intelligence and U.S. House Permanent Select Committee on Intelligence, December 2002, S.Rept. 107-351, H.Rept. 107-792

44 PBS, "The Man Who Knew," *Frontline*, October 3, 2002. Information and transcripts available at *PBS*, http://www.pbs.org/wgbh/pages/frontline/shows/knew/.

45 The second U.S. high-level terrorist planning and response exercise, known as TOPOFF (for top officials) 2, took place in May 2003. The scenario for the exercise was even more ambitious than the previous exercise in 2000, involving the detonation of a radiological device in Seattle, Washington, and a fake threat of a biological weapons attack in Chicago, Illinois. It revealed numerous shortcomings including communications problems, a shortage of medical supplies, and a lack of hospital rooms.

46 "America: Still Unprepared, Still in Danger," report of an independent task force sponsored by the Council on Foreign Relations, Gary Hart and Warren B. Rudman, co-chairs, Stephen E. Flynn, project director, 2002; and "Emergency Responders: Drastically Underfunded, Dangerously Unprepared," report of an independent task force sponsored by the Council on Foreign Relations, Warren B. Rudman, chair, Jamie F. Metzl, project director, 2003.

47 Infrastructure was defined in the first U.S. government analysis of the issue in the 1990s as: "...a network of independent, mostly privately owned, man-made systems and processes that function collaboratively and synergistically to produce and distribute a continuous flow of essential goods and services." In 2003, the USA Patriot Act defines critical infrastructure as "systems and assets, whether physical or virtual, so vital to the United States that the incapacity or destruction of such systems and assets would have a debilitating impact on security, national economic security, national public health or safety, or any combination of those matters."

48 President's Commission on Critical Infrastructure Protection, *Critical Foundations: Protecting America's Infrastructures, The Report of the President's Commission on Critical Infrastructure Protection*, October 1997, http://www.ciao.gov/resource/pccip/report_index.htm.

49 The year 2000, or Y2K, issue refers to problems expected with various computer systems in the year 2000 or later when they try to reconcile the prevailing pre-2000 programming shorthand for years (such as 1984 as 84).

50 The Nanjing Massacre refers to widespread atrocities conducted by Japanese troops against Chinese civilians in Nanjing after its fall in December 1937. Disagreements regarding the extent of these crimes occasionally flare up between certain segments of Japanese and Chinese society.

51 "North Korea Training Hackers, Seoul Says," Reuters, May 16, 2003.

52 The White House, "White Paper: The Clinton Administration's Policy on Critical Infrastructure Protection: Presidential Decision Directive 63" (Washington, D.C., May 22, 1998).

53 Based on discussions with U.S. government officials involved as part of the research for this project.

54 Sarah D. Scalet, "Fear Factor: A Reality Check on Your Top Five Concerns About Reporting Security Incidents," *CIO*, October 15, 2002.

CHAPTER FOUR

Converging
Threats & Responses

✣

There is an element of convergence taking place between the United States and Japan that bodes well for the prospects and potential payoffs of cooperative action above and beyond that already taking place today. The first few decades of the U.S.-Japan post-war relationship were characterized by asymmetry in almost all respects (including economic, military, technological, diplomatic), and it was frequently described as a paternal relationship or one between big brother and little brother. The dynamics of the relationship quickly changed in the 1970s and 1980s and became increasingly competitive in nature. To be sure, there was cooperation on a variety of fronts during those years, particularly in the security arena, but there was also an underlying tension and zero-sum mentality on issues of money (who paid for what) and technology transfer that inhibited broader collaboration. The cooperative atmosphere improved somewhat in the 1990s, but initiatives such as the first Bush administration's U.S.-Japan Global Partnership approach and the Clinton administration's Common Agenda with Japan were often overshadowed by continuing trade conflicts and hampered by Japanese domestic political instability.[55] Today, however, the two countries' interests, approaches, and capabilities are aligned to a degree not seen before in their histories.

The Backdrop: U.S.-Japan Security Cooperation

For both the United States and Japan, crisis and consequence management throughout the Cold War period focused almost exclusively on scenarios arising from that conflict. Immediately after the Cold War, the two allies sought both individually and collectively to ascertain the new threats to their national security and how best to update their capabilities and procedures to counter them. Some of these threats existed during the Cold War, but planning for how to deter and, if necessary, respond to them was considered a lower priority relative to large-scale Cold War contingencies involving the Soviet Union. In East Asia, these included the threats to Japan proper and to U.S. interests posed by China and by North Korea. The end of the Cold War, in some ways, complicated the strategic picture in East Asia, making what was essentially a bipolar and relatively stable corner of the world into a multi-polar and relatively less stable one.

In the United States, the sizing up of the new security environment began during the administration of George H. W. Bush. It was then that the Pentagon devised what became known as the "base force" – a strategy, resource base, and military force structure designed to address the emerging post-Cold War world as it was then perceived. A second, and in some ways more comprehensive, look at the international security environment and the appropriate U.S. national security strategy that should be developed to respond to it, was undertaken by the first secretary of defense in the first Clinton administration, Les Aspin. This effort, the Bottom-Up Review, was issued in October 1993 and was the basis for the Clinton administration's first national security strategy, which in turn was issued in July 1994. Spun off from both the Pentagon's review and the national security strategy were regional strategy documents issued by the civilian side of the Pentagon.

During this time a series of important events took place with regard to North Korea that would affect U.S.-Japan security cooperation significantly for the next decade. In 1993, North Korea test fired its *Nodong* I missile, bringing Japan within missile range, and later ejected international nuclear inspectors while threatening to withdraw from the Nuclear Non-Proliferation Treaty. As former U.S. Defense Secretary William J. Perry and former Assistant Defense Secretary Ashton B. Carter described it, "The two of us spent much of the first half of 1994 preparing for war on the Korean Peninsula…and readied plans for striking North Korea's nuclear facilities and for mobilizing hundreds of thousands of American troops…"[56] President Clinton came very close to authorizing that strike on the Yongbyon nuclear facility, but the attack was avoided after former President Jimmy Carter managed a diplomatic breakthrough with North Korean leader Kim Il Sung that eventually led to a freeze on the North's nuclear program. "We were within a day of making major additions to our troop deployments to Korea, and we were about to undertake an evacuation of American civilians," Perry recalled.[57]

At the time, Japan had little knowledge of how close it actually was to being called upon for significant support in a possible war in Korea. Former Deputy Cabinet Secretary Nobuo Ishihara believed that Japan had dodged a bullet, since the crisis had occurred during a time of domestic political upheaval. "With the poor functioning of the Cabinet," he said "we could not respond to a real crisis."[58] In the United States, military planners began to understand more concretely just how ill prepared the U.S.-Japan alliance was for addressing regional threats in the post-Cold War world. The alliance was designed for a large-scale confrontation with the Soviet Union; it was not ready to handle quick-moving crises, and this sparked a number of changes in the next few years that clarified and codified the specific activities and methods of security and crisis management cooperation.

The February 1995 U.S. strategic document on the East Asia-Pacific region outlined a few of the key issues related to crisis and consequence management in the region for both the United States and Japan.[59] These included the strengthening of key U.S. alliances in the region to refocus on regional post-Cold War challenges and in particular on strengthening the partnership with Japan so that it could help promote both regional and global security. Certain issues were highlighted, such as the potential for problems with North Korea, while others were downplayed, including Taiwan and questions of cooperation on crisis management in response to natural disasters. Interestingly, a photograph in the publication's executive summary shows Japanese SDF personnel unloading blankets donated by USFJ during the Kobe earthquake, attempting to put a positive spin on the roles played by the military forces in both countries in the wake of the disaster and belying the actual lack of a coordinated response. The strategy document itself, however, does not address responding to natural disasters in any way, nor does it discuss how the United States and Japan could cooperate on crisis or consequence management issues per se.

Instead, the strategy document provided the underlying rationale for a broader revitalization of the U.S.-Japan alliance to refocus it on post-Cold War issues in East Asia – mainly, North Korea and Taiwan. It set the stage for the U.S.-Japan Joint Declaration on Security, issued by President Clinton and Prime Minister Hashimoto in April 1996, which in turn initiated a joint review of the 1978 Guidelines for U.S.-Japan Defense Cooperation (Defense Guidelines) to clarify how the allies would work together "in situations in areas surrounding Japan."[60] The revised Defense Guidelines were agreed to by the two allies in the fall of 1997, and they greatly expanded the list of cooperative activities and contingencies for which they would prepare, including disaster relief or dealing with refugees, search and rescue, enforcement of economic sanctions, and logistical and other rear-area support by Japan of U.S. regional operations. The threats that the revised guidelines anticipated were not necessarily new, but the allies had begun to plan for a much more specific menu of contingencies in relation to these primary threats. The new guidelines also laid the groundwork for Japan to draft implementing legislation to empower its SDF to carry out many of these specific missions, thus providing the legal basis for a more versatile and capable complement to American forces in the region. Japan finally adopted the implementing legislation for the revised guidelines in May 1999, roughly five years after the near U.S. air strike on Yongbyon that set the wheels in motion.

More recently, the focus of U.S.-Japan security cooperation has been on implementing and practicing the revised Defense Guidelines. In some cases, such as Japan's naval deployment to the Indian Ocean in support of U.S. and coalition operations in Afghanistan under temporary legislative authority, the allies have gone beyond practice and moved straight to the real thing. In addition, the two countries continue formal discussions on reviewing their respective defense postures in the evolving security environment and meet almost every month under a new consultation mechanism established in 2003 called the Defense Policy Review Initiative (DPRI). The DPRI is an outgrowth of the U.S.-Japan Security Consultative Committee linking the defense and foreign policy teams from both countries (sometimes called the "2+2" meetings), and it provides an opportunity for the allies to discuss on a regular basis such issues as bilateral roles and missions, forces and force structures, and bilateral cooperation in facing regional and global challenges.[61]

Thanks to the North Korean catalyst and a lot of hard work by alliance managers, the United States and Japan have developed a better-equipped toolbox that they can use when a crisis erupts in the region. It should be noted, however, that while many of these new tools could be useful in non-military emergencies, the revised Defense Guidelines are primarily concerned with how the two armed forces (and related government entities) will cooperate in a state-to-state conflict. The differences can be subtle, but they are important. Joint planning for dealing with situations such as evacuating American and Japanese citizens abroad, housing, feeding, and protecting large numbers of refugees, and search and rescue operations can be helpful in the case of a natural or man-made disaster, but it is likely that the mechanisms for initiating cooperation will be different in military and non-military crises, as will the type and number of agencies that could be involved and the complexity of coordination. Moreover, while decision making within a military organization can be relatively quick and clear cut, it is often slow and messy when various bureaucratic and civilian organizations get involved. But quick decision making and clear communication are exactly what will be required, for example, if a terrorist organization arranges the hijacking of an oil supertanker off the coast of Japan. Making effective use of the alliance toolbox in a wider variety of crisis contingencies presents both a challenge and an opportunity for the United States and Japan.

In addition, because so much of the progress in enhancing U.S.-Japan security cooperation was prompted by the threat from North Korea, it is worth considering how the U.S.-Japan alliance might respond to a peaceful process of unification on the peninsula. Thorough analysis of this question could occupy an entire separate study, but for the purposes of this monograph it is enough to suggest that one possible result could be that the allies would place less emphasis on pure military, state-to-state conflict and focus more on general crisis management cooperation and on contributions to overall regional stability, perhaps in a broader, multilateral format.[62]

Clearly, each country has been affected by the growing and changing nature of threats to its policies, citizens, and economy. In addition, changes in the geopolitical environment over the past decade and a half have led to a heightened awareness of certain threats, even if the threats themselves have always been present. As noted in the case studies, lessons have been learned over the years, and some changes in policies, structures, and procedures have been considered and implemented. In the section that follows, a more systematic examination is conducted of the recent changes in the crisis and consequence management systems of Japan and the United States.

Evolution of Crisis Management in Japan

The evolution of Japan's crisis and consequence management policies, procedures, and strategies in the 1990s and first few years of the twenty-first century have brought together two separate strands of change. One is in the security realm, where, as noted above, the United States and Japan jointly negotiated changes to the Defense Guidelines that would allow them to respond more swiftly and efficiently to the changing international environment and the contingencies that could arise. The other is a set of changes in domestic crisis and consequence management triggered by the types of incidents and accidents described in the case studies – earthquakes, industrial accidents, and the Aum Shinrikyo terrorist attack on the Tokyo subway system. One scholar notes that a common thread in the changes, a desire to strengthen leadership capabilities in the country, was the result of the decade-long economic recession that Japan suffered in the 1990s.[63] Institutional and structural changes, many underwritten by new laws, form the basis for understanding Japan's evolution in this issue area.

Institutional and Legal Changes

Shinoda asserts that this desire to strengthen the national political leadership of Japan led to a three-part set of institutional changes that allowed the latest political initiatives in crisis management – Prime Minister Koizumi's anti-terrorism initiatives in the wake of the September 11 attacks on the United States – to take place. The first institutional change, not usually discussed in the context of the Defense Guidelines revisions or other emergency legislation, was the 1994 electoral reform legislation that reduced the power of factions within parties, particularly within the ruling LDP. The second was the government reforms of 1999 aimed at strengthening the role of the cabinet and politicians and at curbing the bureaucracy's influence. The third change, realized in January 2001, was a set of civil service reforms and a consolidation of the bureaucracy within the Cabinet Secretariat and a new cabinet office, making it more responsive to the prime minister.[64]

The most significant institutional changes were designed to enhance the capability of the prime minister to act and to coordinate the various ministries and independent agencies in the Japanese government during a crisis. This is understandable not only in the context of improving decision-making efficiency, but also because the prime minister was increasingly being held accountable by the public for poor performance during times of crisis such as those experienced in Kobe and Tokaimura. There was organizational and political impetus, therefore, for reform throughout the latter half of the 1990s. Change began with the creation of the Cabinet Office for National Security Affairs and

Crisis Management within the prime minister's secretariat in 1998. Legislative support for this change, and the concept behind it of empowering the prime minister's office, was put in place in June 1999 when the cabinet law was revised to strengthen the role of the prime minister and the Cabinet Secretariat in initiating policies of all types. As a result of these two initiatives, this office began to make efforts to improve planning and practice coordination for future crises. It initiated a major interagency exercise in September 2000, named Big Rescue 2000, which focused on a consequence management scenario.

Even this set of reforms, however, was not considered enough, in part because several ministries still held positions of power and influence within the Cabinet Secretariat that could inhibit the prime minister from taking decisive action to prepare for and respond to future crises. In response to this perceived problem, and as part of a larger effort to rein in the Japanese bureaucracy, a further reorganization was undertaken in January 2001 that included changes in crisis management offices and structures. Three policy offices within the Cabinet Secretariat that were run by ministries, including the Cabinet Office for National Security Affairs and Crisis Management, were merged into a single unit, called the Office of Assistant Chief Cabinet Secretaries (ACCS). Many of the staff still comes from other agencies, but in theory they are now more accountable to the prime minister. The idea was to allow some flexibility in how to organize for specific tasks, including crisis management.[65]

In addition to this policy change, information management and decision making were streamlined with the creation, within the Cabinet Secretariat, of a deputy chief cabinet secretary for crisis management (DCCS CM). The DCCS CM takes the lead in a crisis situation and reports to the chief cabinet secretary and the prime minister. He also heads a situation center, an operational entity established after the Kobe earthquake to serve as a central nerve center for information gathering and dispersal. To assist with planning, and to further centralize that function, the Disaster Management Bureau from the National Land Agency was transferred to the Cabinet Office, and the staff of the bureau was increased from thirty-six to fifty. Overseeing broad policy decisions on crisis management issues is the Central Disaster Management Council, a subcommittee of those cabinet ministers with responsibilities or capabilities in the disaster management realm. There is also a plan to further strengthen the Security Council of Japan and to bring some advisory and decision-making functions closer to the prime minister.

Outline Of Japanese Central Government's Crisis/Consequence Management & Preparation Structure

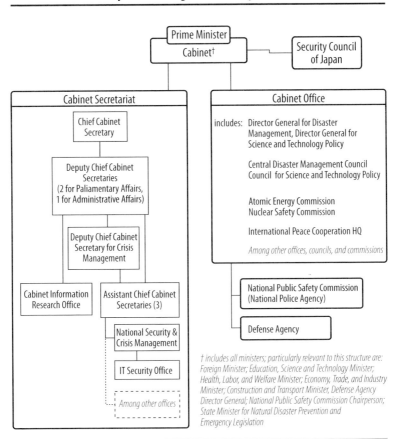

As one can see in the organization chart, the various ministries (in the cabinet), the Cabinet Office, and the Cabinet Secretariat are all part of an integrated policy-making and planning process to prepare for various crises. Once a crisis occurs, however, the center of power shifts dramatically to the Cabinet Secretariat. In a crisis situation, the DCCS CM becomes the point person for coordination, with oversight and support from the deputy chief cabinet secretary for administration (DCCS Admin). Together this team reports to the chief cabinet secretary and prime minister (with input from the other deputy chief cabinet secretaries and certain state ministers, as appropriate to the crisis). The DCCS Admin position is extremely important in the Japanese government, though it tends not to have a high external profile. The DCCS Admin is the liaison between the prime minister and the bureaucracy, and he is often the most frequent visitor to the prime minister's office. Given the relatively short life spans of recent cabinets in Japan, the DCCS Admin post has been exceptionally stable and provided much-needed continuity in policy development and coordination among the successive cabinets and the ministries. Nobuo Ishihara served seven

The Japanese Central Government's Crisis Management Flow Chart

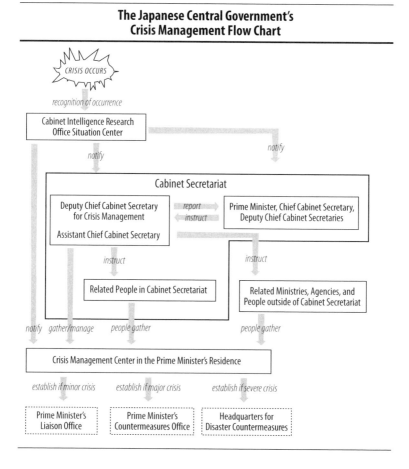

consecutive prime ministers, starting in 1987, and his successor, Teijiro Furukawa, served four: in sixteen years, just two administrative deputies have served eleven prime ministers. A new DCCS Admin, Masahiro Futahashi, joined the Koizumi cabinet in September 2003, so it will be important for U.S. Embassy officials and others in the U.S. government to develop a good relationship with Futahashi and the rest of the Cabinet Secretariat, given the organization's vital role in a crisis situation.

Thus, prodded by a combination of internal forces (public displeasure with the handling of various crises such as Kobe and Tokaimura) and external forces (the changing international environment and U.S. desire to see a more responsive and capable ally), Japan has undergone significant national-level structural changes that should improve its future crisis management capabilities. Reorganizing responsibilities and adjusting organization charts, however, does not mean that Japan's crisis and consequence management problems are over. Some experts have noted continuing shortfalls in the organization and capability of Japan's crisis management structures at the national level, particularly in the area of staffing levels.[66] Moreover, because reforms are relatively new and have been adopted in pieces, further training is needed to improve the network of decision making and information sharing, particularly between the local and central governments. Some additional reforms might also be necessary to stitch this patchwork together into a more seamless and efficient operation. Many of the staff who work in the Cabinet Office or Cabinet Secretariat on these issues are on loan from other agencies and ministries (such as the NPA, Defense Agency, MOFA, or METI) and otherwise retain a certain amount of loyalty to, or bureaucratic habits from, their former office. The United States faces similar challenges as it glues together various departments and agencies into the new DHS.

Additionally, there is some competition between agencies and ministries for influence in these new structures. For years there had been an unwritten rule in Tokyo that, in order to prevent confusion in the flow of information, organizations that handle intelligence such as the NPA, Public Security Investigation Agency (PSIA), and Defense Agency (but excluding

MOFA), provided intelligence through a centralized channel to the cabinet information officer and not directly to the prime minister. The threat from North Korea and bureaucratic changes, however, appear to have destroyed this unwritten rule, and the heads of these three agencies have frequently visited the prime minister in the first eight months of 2003 (NPA three times, PSIA six times, and Defense Agency seven times). One government official called it "a fierce battle for leadership," and an officer in charge of intelligence lamented, "If this anarchic situation [in intelligence handling] continues, the government could make a serious mistake in judgment."[67] These kinds of turf battles are common during periods of reform in any country, so while leaders need to remain vigilant during this process to improve clarity and efficiency, we should not lose sight of the accomplishments that Japan has made in the area of crisis management decision making.

The Koizumi administration took advantage of the stronger cabinet structures to respond swiftly after the September 11 attacks on the United States, but it also realized that new laws would be necessary to enact all of the measures it had in mind. Koizumi, therefore, resuscitated draft bills that had been studied over twenty-five years ago detailing how Japan would react in the case of an armed attack and other scenarios. The bills were controversial and were the subject of much debate and some compromise in the cabinet before being submitted to the Diet for consideration in April 2002. It took another year of debate before the Diet approved these three pieces of national emergency legislation in June 2003. The passage came only after significant compromise among the three parties of the ruling bloc and the largest opposition party, including inserting provisions into the legislation that supported the protection of human rights and freedom of speech during future emergencies. Another external catalyst, the winter/spring 2003 crisis with North Korea over its nuclear weapons capabilities, gave the final impetus necessary for passage.[68] A summary of the bills is seen in the accompanying text box.

The newly passed national emergency legislation in Japan begins to clarify two key issues long in need of consideration: the

A Summary of the Three National Emergency Bills Passed in June 2003

1. **Bill to Respond to Armed Attack Situation.** Prescribes the basic principles for response to an armed attack on Japan (or "anticipated attack"), the respective responsibilities of the national and local governments, and the areas in which the public will need to cooperate. The cabinet will decide how to respond, with prior approval of the Diet, but the law permits ex post facto approval in an urgent situation.
2. **Bill to Amend the Self-Defense Forces Law.** Corrects long-standing, pending legislative issues regarding the activities of the SDF, such as land use and exempting the SDF from the governing Road Law in an armed attack situation, and other details.
3. **Bill to Amend the Law on Establishment of the Security Council of Japan.** This amendment would strengthen the functions of the Security Council of Japan in the event of a national emergency.[69]

role of central authorities vis-à-vis local officials and the role of the military in a crisis and consequence management situation. It should now be easier for the prime minister to control events at the local level in an emergency, and the SDF will also have greater freedom to do what it needs to do in order to protect local citizens, leverage local resources, or pursue intruders. These improvements are all incremental, however, and much additional work remains. In many ways the new laws are only a beginning and not an end in terms of organizing for better crisis and consequence management. There are still questions regarding the military's potential use of port facilities and airports, for example, among other outstanding issues. Most relevant to this study is the plan to clarify the SDF's interaction with the U.S. military during an emergency. According to MOFA, it plans to work with the Cabinet Secretariat, the Defense Agency, and other relevant authorities to draft new legislation with a special emphasis on "measures to facilitate the smooth action of the U.S. military in the case of an armed attack against Japan or other such emergency."[70] There will be controversial aspects of the new legislation, and for good reason the bills should be thoughtfully considered and thoroughly debated in Japan. The United States can do more than just be a spectator in this process, but it is not necessary (indeed, it could be harmful) for the U.S. government to inject itself forcefully into the discussion. The most constructive role the United States can play is to contribute generously to the drafting process as requested, to be available in public forums and inform the debate, and to monitor the bureaucratic struggle carefully so that it can quietly lobby at appropriate times to protect its own interests and help promote a rational, efficient, and effective piece of legislation.

Throughout this process of upgrading the national crisis management system in Japan, authorities will also need to continue paying attention to local-level capabilities, structures, and procedures. In general, large cities and national capitals have the best local disaster response capabilities, but, as was shown in the Kobe and Tokaimura tragedies, disaster can strike anywhere, and Japan's local and prefecture-level organization, plans, and capabilities should not be overlooked. Tokyo's emergency management capabilities today are quite impressive, and national-level exercises tend to focus – naturally – on the capital. Despite the obvious improvements at the national level, it remains to be seen if national-level policy guidance, and supporting funds, will trickle down to the prefecture and local levels. While the new emergency legislation mandates more specific roles and responsibilities for local and prefecture officials, ensuring that these roles are well understood and that local capabilities are well funded and exercised regularly is a challenge. In addition, the operational connection for crisis management with the military – either the SDF or USFJ – often takes place at the local level. These are issues faced by the United States, as well.

The Military

The role of Japan's SDF in crisis and consequence management has long been less robust than one would expect, primarily because of historical sensitivity about the military's participation in policy and society in Japan. This role began to evolve over the course of the 1990s – after subdued debate that began decades before – in large part to respond to changes in the international environment after the Cold War. As noted above, the successful negotiation and implementation of the Guidelines for U.S.-Japan Defense Cooperation was a major step to allowing the Japanese military to play a larger role in future contingencies in and around Japan.[71] In addition, one of the lessons learned from the Kobe earthquake was that local coordination and cooperation with the SDF were inadequate, and that therefore capabilities the SDF could have brought to bear on the crisis were not effectively utilized.

Since the Kobe earthquake and the passage of laws implementing the 1997 revised Defense Guidelines, the SDF has begun – slowly – to be integrated more systematically into crisis and consequence management preparations. SDF participation in a Tokyo-area disaster response exercise grew substantially in 2000 during Big Rescue Tokyo 2000. Some seven thousand SDF troops joined the exercise, compared to about five hundred the year before. The operation pretended that an earthquake with a magnitude of 7.2 (Richter) struck the capital during the morning rush hour. The exercise cost about $2.8 million to carry out and involved over twenty-five thousand people.[72] The SDF has continued to participate in subsequent exercises of this type, with Big Rescue 2001 testing the coordination between national- and prefecture-level governments, the fire departments, police, the SDF, and volunteers in a Tokyo earthquake scenario. The 2001 exercise also marked the first time that the USFJ air base in Yokota was used as a connection and transit hub. Tokyo Governor Ishihara has long insisted that the Yokota base be used not only by the U.S. military, but also by civilians, and he would apparently ask the United States to use the facility in case of a real disaster.[73] Nationwide, over two million people participated in the 2001 drills, organized by forty-four prefectural governments.[74]

The presence of SDF vehicles in downtown Tokyo during the 2000 exercise was apparently a bit of a shock to a portion of the population, and some accused Governor Ishihara of pushing larger-than-necessary SDF involvement to make a political statement about the role of the military in Japanese society. Indeed, SDF personnel participated in smaller numbers (around two thousand) in the 2001 exercise compared to the year before. In general, however, the stepped-up profile of the SDF in these drills did not generate as much negative reaction as would likely have been the case in decades past, and its involvement is vital for Japan to leverage all available resources in a time of crisis. Going forward, SDF participation in similar exercises should always be driven by need as determined by crisis management professionals, and it should be neither promoted nor restricted for political reasons. In addition, more local governments should look to incorporate SDF assets in their disaster management planning. Very few local governments besides Tokyo have taken this initiative. One exception is Tottori Prefecture, where Governor Yoshihiro Katayama orchestrated an emergency response simulation in July 2003 and developed an evacuation plan in collaboration with local SDF, police, and fire officials.

Cooperation between the SDF (and national crisis management planners) and USFJ has evolved as well. USFJ operates in Japan under a status of forces agreement (SOFA) that requires them to obey Japanese laws. Although it is so far unclear how follow-on bills to the recently passed national emergency legislation will allow U.S. forces, if so requested by Japanese authorities, to respond more fully in support of crisis and/or consequence management tasks, some mechanisms already exist for formal coordination between USFJ and the Japanese government during a crisis. Moreover, there are plans to enhance this bilateral coordination mechanism (BCM) to cover more explicitly a wider array of crisis and consequence management situations.

Within the BCM, the Japan-U.S. Joint Committee coordinates policy on issues related to the SOFA, and the Japan-U.S. Policy Committee handles non-SOFA issues. The two committees work together as the Joint Coordination Group in times of crisis and coordinate their respective military actions, which are managed operationally by USFJ and the SDF at a bilateral coordination center (BCC). Formal requests for assistance in a disaster are traditionally passed by the government of Japan to the U.S. government through the U.S. Embassy in Tokyo. However, if the crisis is occurring in an area where U.S. forces are based or deployed in Japan, there is a good chance that the local commander will have a better understanding of the requirements, and, once authority is given, can respond swiftly and efficiently. In addition, local U.S. base commanders

Bilateral Coordination Mechanism Structure

Japan-U.S. Joint Committee			Japan-U.S. Policy Committee	
Japanese Side	**U.S. Side**	**Primary Responsibility**	**Japanese Side**	**U.S. Side**
Director-General of North American Affairs Bureau, Ministry of Foreign Affairs, etc.,	Deputy Commander of USFJ		Bureau Chief Level Representatives from Cabinet Sectretariat, Ministry of Foreign Affairs, and Defense Agency/SDF	Bureau Chief Level Representatives from Department of State, U.S. Embassy in Japan, Department of Defense and USFJ
policy coordination on matters beyond the scope of the Japan-U.S. Joint Committee			Representatives from other relevant ministries, if necessary	
			policy coordination on matters beyond the scope of the Japan-U.S. Joint Committee	

Joint Coordination Group
(Guidelines Task Force/Steering Committee)

Japanese Side	U.S. Side
Division Chief Level Representatives from Cabinet Sectretariat, Ministry of Foreign Affairs, and Defense Agency/SDF	Division Chief Level Representatives from Department of State, U.S. Embassy in Japan and USFJ
Representatives from other relevant ministries, if necessary	

- The Guideline Task Force is set up under the Japan-U.S. Joint Committee and the Steering Committee under the Japan-U.S. Policy Committee.
- The two function as one group and coordinate the activities of both the SDF and USFJ as well as matters that require the involvement of relevant organizations in Japan or the U.S.

mutual coordination and information exchange

Japanese Side	U.S. Side
Representatives from Joint Staff Council and Staff Offices of each SDF service	Representatives from USFJ Headquarters
coordination of activities of both the SDF and USFJ	

maintain direct liaison relationships with local and prefecture officials. The trilateral coordination among these three groups – local SDF commanders/units, local USFJ units/bases, and local civilian officials – is important and needs to be practiced on a regular basis. Critical issues such as the actual plans for reception of U.S. forces to join in crisis response are still in the conceptual stage, and rigorous exercises have yet to occur. As an SDF officer noted at a 2002 project conference on this subject, "Without practice, the manual on how to respond is useless."[75] The next few years are an important window of opportunity for improving and enhancing joint SDF-USFJ crisis and consequence management capabilities.

The SDF has also been expanding its capabilities to handle different types of pure military situations. One example is its recent push to acquire capabilities to deal with a guerrilla-commando or special operation incursion into Japan. The main consideration here is the potential for an assault or terrorist attack of some kind launched by an intruding North Korean spy boat with commando troops. Specific guerrilla-commando exercises began in 2000, and in 2001 involved a Japan-U.S. joint field exercise in Hokkaido with marines from Okinawa.[76] The SDF is also considering the creation of a standing unit of SDF dedicated to peacekeeping, anti-terrorism, and other overseas operations.[77] There are about nineteen hundred SDF personnel currently serving on missions abroad, but Japan does not yet have a centralized mechanism of command and coordination for those forces. In addition, Japan has branched out beyond its work with U.S. forces and signed a memorandum with Australia in September 2003 for cooperation on counter-terrorism and counter-proliferation. Japan has also presented an initiative to ASEAN for greater regional cooperation on these issues. Japan and Australia, together with the United States and other countries, have already carried out joint exercises in the Coral Sea to stop nations such as North Korea from exporting missile and nuclear-weapons technology.[78]

Consequence Management for Weapons of Mass Destruction

Many of the changes and upgrades made to crisis management procedures, processes, and capabilities apply to any situation, regardless of the nature of the incident. However, consequence management for incidents involving WMD requires specialized capabilities. In Japan, the subject of WMD, particularly nuclear weapons, carries with it a political stigma, and therefore preparing for incidents of this type has long been considered politically unpalatable. The Aum Shinrikyo attack on the Tokyo subway using sarin gas was a wakeup call for both Japan and the United States, but some analysts believe that the United States took the incident more seriously than the government of Japan and made appropriate adjustments in threat assumptions, plans, and capabilities.[79] The government of Japan, however, did make several revisions to its crisis management plans, institutions, and procedures specifically with future WMD events in mind.[80]

Even after the sarin gas attack, public discussion of WMD attacks and the requirement for consequence management capabilities remains muted in Japan. The SDF has, over time, improved its chemical and biological detection and response capabilities. A special Defense Agency panel on biological weapons countermeasures issued a report in 2001 that formed the basis for a stronger national commitment to preparing for and countering biological weapons. The Ground SDF takes the lead in chemical situations, and now has over 670 personnel in fifteen units deployed all over Japan. Shortfalls remain, however, if only in an understanding by officials of the units' capabilities (as the dispatch of the ill-prepared Chemical Protection Unit to Tokaimura showed). Laws were passed that prohibited activities such as those Aum carried out, enabling police to be more proactive when threats of this type by religious groups are detected. Planning for mass casualty attacks involving WMD has begun at various hospitals, but the activities remain uneven across major facilities. Coordination on these issues with the United States has improved, but given the time-criticality of WMD events, any support that Washington might provide – whether from Japan-based forces or from those flown into the country – would be supplementary. The primary responsibility would obviously rest with Japanese civilian and military organizations. The ongoing crisis with North Korea, and Pyongyang's now-declared nuclear potential, may provide new impetus in Japan for more concentrated effort on consequence management, as it has with consideration of a national missile defense capability.

Critical Infrastructure and Cyber Security

As noted earlier, critical infrastructure protection – and especially cyber security – relies to an almost inordinate degree on the actions of the private sector as opposed to government entities. Out of former Prime Minister Hashimoto's initiative on an advanced information society, the Japanese government has – in conjunction with its broader strengthening of the prime minister's office and the cabinet and its secretariat – built an overarching government structure to address the issue of what it calls "IT security." The basic structure is outlined below. Overall policy direction is given by the IT Strategy Headquarters, which is headed by the prime minister and is an outgrowth of the desire to have Japan take full advantage of information age technology. Under the IT Strategy Headquarters, two subordinate entities – one consisting of a committee of directors general from the various ministries with interest in the subject and another of private sector experts – coordinate and exchange information on security issues. Policy planning, design, and integration are carried out in the IT Security Office within the Cabinet Secretariat, with input from the two aforementioned committees. Out of the IT Security Office and the IT Security Promotion Committee, interagency coordination is achieved. Private-sector liaison and communication are achieved through two outlets: the IT Security Expert Meeting and the direct and long-stand-

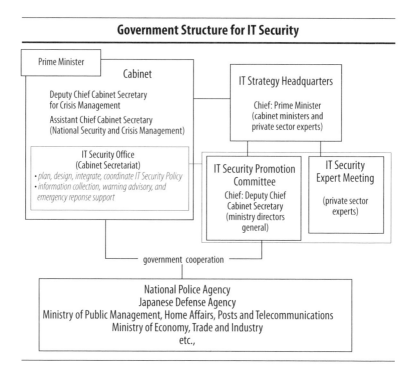

Government Structure for IT Security

Prime Minister

Cabinet

Deputy Chief Cabinet Secretary
for Crisis Management

Assistant Chief Cabinet Secretary
(National Security and Crisis Management)

IT Security Office
(Cabinet Secretariat)
• plan, design, integrate, coordinate IT Security Policy
• information collection, warning advisory, and
emergency reponse support

IT Strategy Headquarters

Chief: Prime Minister
(cabinet ministers and
private sector experts)

IT Security Promotion
Committee

Chief: Deputy Chief
Cabinet Secretary
(ministry directors
general)

IT Security
Expert Meeting

(private sector
experts)

government cooperation

National Police Agency
Japanese Defense Agency
Ministry of Public Management, Home Affairs, Posts and Telecommunications
Ministry of Economy, Trade and Industry
etc.,

ing relationships that the various ministries have with the industries they regulate.

As noted in chapter 3, Japan responded to the new challenge in the arena of cyber security with a combination of structural reform that gave the policy lead to the prime minister and the Cabinet Secretariat and new legal authorities. Despite the focus of policy making in the Cabinet Secretariat, the individual ministries still control much of the policy implementation and retain the resources and connections necessary to bring the Japanese private sector up to speed on the requirements for improved cyber security. Some Japanese officials indicate that the connections with the private sector still require significant work and that the weak economy makes any costly improvement of cyber security difficult. Much like the United States, Japan began organizing on the cyber security issue nationally and has only recently reached out in a more systematic way internationally.

Evolution of Crisis Management in the United States

The most significant development in U.S. crisis and consequence management since the end of the Cold War was the decision by President Bush on June 6, 2002, to establish the cabinet-level Department of Homeland Security. After ten months of attempting to coordinate efforts at the White House for detection and deterrence of terrorism on the one hand and crisis and consequence management on the other, the Bush administration came to the conclusion that a separate cabinet department was needed to pull the various authorities and capabilities together under one bureaucratic entity. The DHS has a military counterpart, Northern Command, which will manage homeland defense.[82] Internationally, the DoD has also been looking critically at past approaches and arrangements, a practice begun even before September 11. It has been moving toward a revised strategy for basing troops and equipment overseas, which could have implications for the composition of U.S. forces in Japan and in the region as a whole. The United States has also embraced certain multilateral approaches for both military and non-military threats, tailored to the situation at hand (for example, in the areas of cyber security, counter-terrorism, counter-proliferation, and search and rescue). U.S. multilateral approaches, however, have been inconsistent, and it is not yet clear how they will be pursued under the new bureaucratic arrangements.

U.S. Homeland Security and Reform

The new DHS pulled together a variety of existing federal agencies and offices under one roof, reporting to the secretary for homeland security and consolidating the budget process for these activities. The DHS was officially created on January 24, 2003, though most components of the department were not transferred under DHS authority until March, and the transfer process for all 170,000 employees was not fully completed until October 1, 2003. On that day, President Bush signed the first-ever DHS appropriations bill, totaling $37.6 billion for the fiscal year 2004.

DHS activities are primarily carried out by four major directorates: 1) Border and Transportation Security (U.S. Customs Service, part of the Immigration and Naturalization Service, Transportation Security Administration, and other components); 2) Emergency Preparedness and Response (including FEMA, Strategic National Stockpile and the National Disaster Medical System, and the Nuclear Incident Response Team); 3) Science and Technology (Chemical, Biological, Radiological and Nuclear (CBRN) Countermeasures, Plum Island Animal Disease Center, and other facilities); and 4) Information Analysis and Infrastructure Protection (including the CIAO, Federal Computer Incident Response Center, and National Cyber Security Division). The Secret Service and the Coast Guard are also located in the department and report directly to the secretary. Despite the fact that DHS was essentially cobbled together from other departments' agencies and offices (e.g., from Treasury, Justice, Energy, Agriculture, Transportation, Commerce, and Defense), the management and coordination functions within the DHS are brand new, and many jobs remain vacant as its work begins. The jobs that are filled are usually by staff from other agencies and departments, either as "detailees" (one-year assignment to DHS as a temporary DHS employee) or "liaisons" (still paid by, and representing, their home department). Moreover, the DHS is still in the early stages of designing and communicating the details of its policies, objectives, and priorities. As in Japan, now is an important time of governmental organizational history that will influence many aspects of the department's future culture and relationships.

The new DHS has a simple, threefold mission: 1) to prevent terrorist attacks on the United States; 2) to reduce America's vulnerability to terrorism; and 3) to minimize the damage from potential attacks and natural disasters.[83] For some components of the new department, such as the Coast Guard or FEMA, this mission transition is a relatively small jump. For others, however, it is transformational. The Customs Bureau is a good example of an agency where domestic security concerns coexisted with or were subordinate to other priorities such as facilitating commerce or looking for illegal drugs. Efforts to speed customs clearance times and streamline paperwork will continue, but not at the expense of its primary missions. The Transportation Security Administration is another example, since it will not

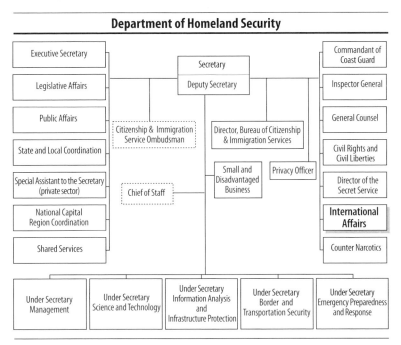

need to balance security costs against the costs to the air or rail industries (or customers) in the same way it would within the Department of Transportation. Looking at its collective work through the lens of homeland security, the DHS will redirect the investment of public funds based on these new priorities.

Given this "homeland" focus, the department starts out with a heavy domestic bias, but it is also widely recognized that domestic security is inextricably linked to the broader global community and international developments. The Bureau of Customs and Border Protection (CBP), for example, has a specific Container Security Initiative Division within its Office of International Affairs to extend its perimeter of defense to ports overseas. The United States and Japan agreed to a declaration of principles on the subject in September 2002, and announced in March 2003 that the Container Security Initiative was operational at the port of Yokohama for cargo containers bound for U.S. ports. The agreement allows a small team of CBP officers to work at the port of Yokohama and screen containers for potential terrorist risks, in cooperation with Japanese port officials. The initiative went into effect at the ports of Tokyo, Nagoya, and Kobe in subsequent months. Together, those four Japanese ports account for almost 10 percent of all sea containers arriving in the United States. The initiative also allows for Japanese customs personnel to be stationed at U.S. ports. Fourteen other ports around the world have also signed on to this initiative, which demonstrates the ability of nations to cooperate quickly and effectively when priorities align (the commercial driver of access to U.S. markets does not hurt either). The record is less impressive, however, when the benefits of cooperation are less obvious or where the habits of international cooperation are relatively weak.

The organizational challenges faced by the new DHS are daunting. Imagine assembling a company the size of Fujitsu or Federal Express (FedEx) in one year, stitched together from dozens of smaller companies and corporate cultures. Yet while most observers recognize these hurdles, the DHS is unlikely to receive a grace period, given the potentially serious consequences for any breakdowns in performance. DHS leadership is therefore understandably focused on the nation's most pressing vulnerabilities and preoccupied with internal organization. The Coast Guard and the CBP Bureau have international liaison offices and active outreach programs, but these were inherited from their previous structures and brought established international networks with them. There is also a small Office of International Affairs that reports directly to the secretary of homeland security, and although its resources are limited, it could become a valuable means of information exchange between the United States and its allies.[84]

The DHS Office of International Affairs has four major functions: 1) to promote information and education exchange with friendly nations to share best practices and technologies related to homeland security (including joint training of joint responders and exchange of terrorism prevention and crisis management expertise); 2) to identify areas of homeland security where the United States has a demonstrated weakness and an ally has a corresponding strength; 3) to carry out international conferences and exchange programs; and 4) to manage international activities within the department in coordination with other U.S. officials responsible for counter-terrorism. The issue of department coordination is important, and the DHS-State Department relationship in particular will need clarification over time. The State Department will always be the lead agency with respect to foreign affairs, but the details can be more complicated than just that. For example, with regard to the above mission of the DHS International Affairs Office, when it comes to counter-terrorism, the State Department has the lead in any activity that helps a foreign government combat terrorism, and the DHS has the lead if the activity helps the United States. Mutually beneficial exchanges, therefore, fall into a gray area where both departments will probably be involved. Clarifying these types of issues can sometimes be done informally, as habits of cooperation and consultation take hold, but in other cases further reform might be necessary. One example of the latter is the recent signing of a formal memorandum of understanding between the two departments regarding visa oversight.[85]

Three other directorates (Emergency Preparedness and Response, Information Analysis and Infrastructure Protection, and Science and Technology) do not have formal structures to develop specific objectives for international cooperation or interacting with foreign governments beyond ad hoc relationships that have been carried over at the office level. For example, a government strategy paper in the area of cyber security (an issue with numerous global connections) concludes with forty-seven actions and recommendations, but only six of those forty-seven involve international cooperation.[86] Moreover, there is no clear mechanism for the Information Analysis and Infrastructure Protection Directorate to engage foreign partners on these matters. Some of these initiatives can be carried out by the directorate, others by the DHS Office of International Affairs, and all must be done in cooperation with the State Department. It remains to be seen whether or not foreign governments should work primarily with the State Department (either in Washington or through the resident embassy) on these issues, or directly with the DHS, or the Commerce Department, or all three. Deciding on and opening up the channels of communication between the United States and Japan will pay dividends in the future, but some investment of time and leadership is required to consider and guide the process.

As in Japan, creating new bureaucratic structures in the United States has led to varying degrees of policy infighting and organizational competition for influence and power, especially since the new structures draw resources from other departments. Before the DHS was formally established and funded, for example, the Department of Health and Human Services (HHS) had the honor of funneling about $1 billion to local communities to fight bioterrorism. Today, however, the DHS oversees many of the same programs and has responsibility for deploying HHS's stockpiles of vaccines in an emergency, even though some in HHS complain that the DHS does not have enough medical and healthcare expertise to manage the programs properly. Others lament that too much of the precious federal funding has been allocated to local fire and police forces at the expense of other first responders such as hospitals, doctors, and nurses.[87] Cyber security and critical infrastructure protection are also delicate issues for the DHS, since so many of its initiatives require close cooperation with the private sector, and the Commerce and Energy Departments dominate those private sector relationships. Government leaders must do everything they can to discourage a zero-sum mentality between the bureaucratic organizations. Similar to many of the changes taking place in Japan, the standing up of a new DHS in the United States represents a beginning and not an end to the process of crisis and consequence management reform.

U.S. Military

At the same time that the DHS began its first full fiscal year of operation, its military cousin, the U.S. Northern Command (NORTHCOM), was officially established. NORTHCOM was created after the 2002 biennial review of the Unified Command Plan.[88] Its primary mission is to deter and defeat threats and aggression aimed at the United States in its area of responsibility, which includes the continental United States, Canada, Mexico, and parts of the Caribbean. NORTHCOM's secondary mission is to provide military assistance to civil authorities, including consequence management operations. Political sensitivities and some legal restrictions in the United States regarding the military's involvement in law enforcement activities force the government to be careful in how it explains the role of NORTH-COM. NORTHCOM does not have a direct tie to the DHS (it is answerable only to DoD and the president), it does not oversee law enforcement (Department of Justice), secure airports or borders (DHS), or provide first responders (local governments). It does, however, have resources available to track all aircraft and ships in the region, conduct training for pilots and other forces to intercept potential attacks, and manage the dispatch of troops to help in case of natural disasters. Even though NORTHCOM has only been in existence for a short while, it has already sent military personnel to help fight wildfires in California and assisted in tracking Hurricane Isabel in 2003. NORTHCOM has a modest $81 million annual budget, underscoring its narrow coordination and command functions, as opposed to being an operational arm of the military. The relevance of NORTHCOM to this study is that the United States now has a command structure with an overall mission somewhat similar to that of Japan's SDF, which was not the case before, and it highlights the convergence taking place in both countries' crisis and consequence management systems.

More relevant to the issue of U.S.-Japan crisis management cooperation in a military context are changes in strategic approach and resource allocation taking place or under consideration with respect to U.S. forces and the fight against terrorism around the world. The changes are multi-faceted, but the end result could be a more dispersed and flexible U.S. military infrastructure that seeks to leverage the resources of steadfast allies for collective benefit through finely tuned agreements on roles, responsibilities, and investments. Homeland defense has obviously taken on significant priority in U.S. planning, and this has produced a new organizing principle based on a layered-defense concept. At the outermost layer, the United States would deter aggres-

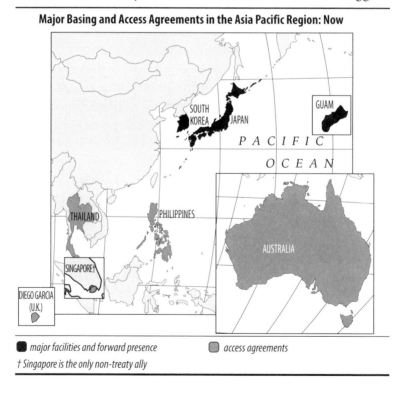

Major Basing and Access Agreements in the Asia Pacific Region: Now

■ *major facilities and forward presence*   ▢ *access agreements*

† *Singapore is the only non-treaty ally*

sion and defend its interests with forward-deployed forces, with NORTHCOM and military support of U.S. civil authorities as the second and third layers respectively. Related to this is the abandonment of the two-major-theater-war construct, which in turn has implications for the needs of, and training parameters for, U.S. bases overseas.[89]

In the U.S.-Japan context, this suggests that a more detailed examination of roles and missions for the alliance is needed, in part because a clearer understanding of each side's tasks would reduce redundant investments in key capabilities, such as strategic lift and reconnaissance. Bilateral interagency coordination mechanisms can also be created for a range of traditional and non-traditional activities, such as intelligence sharing, commu-

Major Basing and Access Agreements in the Asia Pacific Region: In the Future?

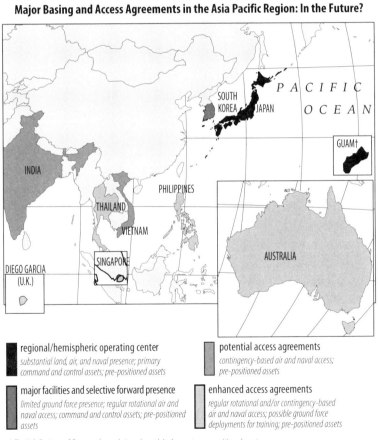

▮ regional/hemispheric operating center
substantial land, air, and naval presence; primary command and control assets; pre-positioned assets

▮ potential access agreements
contingency-based air and naval access; pre-positioned assets

▮ major facilities and selective forward presence
limited ground force presence; regular rotational air and naval access; command and control assets; pre-positioned assets

▮ enhanced access agreements
regular rotational and/or contingency-based air and naval access; possible ground force deployments for training; pre-positioned assets

† The U.S. Territory of Guam: enhanced air and naval deployments; pre-positioned assets

nications support, contingency planning, training, and joint exercises. In this context, expanding the joint use of bases in Japan and further increasing interoperability could contribute to a more flexible and efficient security arrangement, though all of this would represent a significant investment of time (and in some cases, political capital) to agree upon and implement. The current trend for the alliance is moving in this direction, but time will tell how much effort the allies will be willing to devote to this objective, given other priorities. The DPRI meetings are an encouraging sign on this point, as long as senior leaders stay closely involved in the discussions and the public is eventually brought into the debate.

As noted earlier, the 1997 revised Defense Guidelines focused the two countries on detailed planning for joint operations in the area surrounding Japan (for situations that affect Japan's security), but it is only in the last two or three years that the planning and exercises under the new rubric have taken on a concrete form. The BCM, called for in the guidelines, was not established until 2000, and it took more time to carry out formal operational exercises utilizing the BCC. Two Japan-U.S. joint, integrated command post exercises were conducted in 2002, and the level of integration and sophistication increases with every effort. In February, about sixty U.S. personnel from Hickam Air Force Base in Hawaii deployed to Yokota Air Base in Japan to practice "split operations" with the Japanese, a technique to rapidly deploy people with fewer aircraft and creating a smaller footprint in a forward air operations center by using technology to link back to the home base.[90] The allies are also practicing larger-scale operations, as in November 2002 for an assumed outbreak of a "situation in areas surrounding Japan." Together they conducted search-and-rescue operations, transported Japanese from areas of conflict, and performed ship inspections for economic sanctions. The exercise involved about eleven thousand personnel, twenty vessels, and 180 aircraft from Japan's SDF, and over ten thousand personnel, ten vessels, and 150 aircraft from U.S. forces. Japanese ships were assigned to escort the U.S. carrier *Kitty Hawk,* and the two forces also practiced air operation coordination through a "merged" command at Tsuiki

Air base.[91] The two countries have also begun to explore ways to apply the BCM/BCC process to a broader range of crisis situations (including large earthquakes), though progress in this area will likely lag behind discussions on further refinements to the national emergency legislation.

All of these plans and exercises are intended for crises of national security for Japan or for internationally sanctioned peace and security missions, because of Japan's ongoing adherence to an interpretation of its constitution that Japan cannot exercise its right of collective self-defense. This limitation that Japan can only respond in an emergency that directly and specifically threatens Japan is becoming increasingly problematic for defense and crisis management planners. Even small (almost innocuous) but prudent steps are often cause for lengthy debate before implementation or undue scandal after the fact. For example, after the September 11 attacks, the U.S. Navy stepped up patrols in the waters around vulnerable U.S. vessels in the navy's Sasebo base in Japan, and Maritime SDF personnel joined those patrols to facilitate communication and extend protection to Japanese ships in the harbor. This activity took place, however, before legislation was approved to allow Japan's SDF to help guard USFJ facilities, and it has been argued by some as violating the nation's prohibition of collective self-defense.[92]

The hair splitting over such issues in Tokyo can sometimes border on the ridiculous as policy makers try to justify when a particular action might be warranted. Could Japan respond preemptively to a feared North Korean missile attack if the North was clearly preparing a launch and aiming its missile toward Japan, or would Tokyo have to wait until Pyongyang fired the missile to confirm its trajectory and whether it was headed for Japan (in which case it could try to intercept) or Hawaii (when it technically should not intercept)? Will Japan have to justify helping the United States interdict North Korean freighters on a case-by-case basis, depending on how much evidence there is that the cargo threatens Japan? The Japanese government seems to agree that the country can and should find a way to exercise its right of collective self-defense without undermining its exclusively defense-oriented posture and still remain faithful to the constitution. A MOFA panel, headed by University of Tokyo professor Shinichi Kitaoka, recently completed a year-long study that concluded, "The government's interpretation of the Constitution, barring the country from exercising the right of collective defense, is an obstacle."[93] Japan should pursue an open, legal process to remove this obstacle while maintaining its fundamental constitutional principles. A constitutional amendment would be the most legitimate option in this regard.

There is also an increased interest in conducting certain multilateral exercises, be they directed at countering proliferation of WMD (as in the Bush administration's Proliferation Security Initiative alluded to above) or rescuing disabled submarines. The first such regional submarine rescue exercise took place in the Pacific in October 2000 and involved ships from the United States, Japan, South Korea, and Singapore, with several other countries joining as observers. This kind of multinational naval exercise is becoming more common and will improve the countries' ability to respond to a crisis at sea in the future, as long as political considerations do not frustrate a consensus. Japan even briefly joined in Russia's largest naval exercise in five years in August 2003, along with a South Korean destroyer and a U.S. Coast Guard vessel, focused on various anti-terrorism and rescue maneuvers. China, Canada, and South Korea sent a few observers. These are prudent steps that should continue to be promoted and coordinated. There will be occasions when sensitive political issues are involved that will complicate multilateral cooperation (e.g., any issue involving disputed territory such as Taiwan or what Japan calls the Northern Territories),[94] but there are enough non-controversial contingencies worth preparing for that could minimize adverse impacts and strengthen the overall security environment.

U.S.-Japan Cooperation in a Multilateral Context

Although the main focus of this study is on bilateral cooperation, it is important to note that such cooperation can and should take place within a multilateral context as well. In some cases, multilateral cooperation will be the primary avenue for dealing with such issues as cyber security or controlling the spread of epidemic diseases, and it can also play an important role in addressing problems of terrorism (particularly bioterrorism), WMD proliferation, energy security (oil shipping and pipelines), and the aftermath of natural disasters in poorer countries. For the sake of narrowing the scope of discussion, this section will briefly note developments in two promising areas for bilateral leadership and the coordination of multilateral cooperation: cyber security and bioterrorism.

As mentioned earlier, the United States and Japan have been pursuing bilateral cooperation in a multilateral context for several years, largely beginning with the Reagan and George H. W. Bush administrations (culminating in the U.S.-Japan Global Partnership) and in the Clinton administration with the U.S.-Japan Common Agenda. In George W. Bush's administration one hears little or no mention of the Common Agenda, but the two countries continue to cooperate on global and regional concerns related to the environment, economic development, and public health in much the same manner and spirit as before. The GWOT, however, has brought other security problems into sharper focus, and as a result has blurred the lines that more clearly divided security and non-security cooperation before the September 11 attacks. What were previously separate avenues of cooperation (such as security, commerce, development assistance, and health) are in a sense merging into a broader boulevard of issues that will frequently influence crisis and consequence management planning. Until now, the private and public sectors in both countries have been accustomed to dealing with their respective issues in relatively narrow terms and with a limited number of counterparts. The challenge from now on will be for bureaucracies and companies to keep pace with the changes and share more lessons and connections across disciplines.

Cyber security and critical infrastructure protection are examples of this phenomenon, though the issues' origins stem less from September 11 than they do from wider trends in business practices and technological development. Still, the GWOT has significantly affected the approach to the issues and the placement of priorities. Tracking terrorist financing, for example, is as much a part of the cyber security debate as stopping troublesome hackers. With regard to law enforcement, the United States and Japan moved quickly in 2002 to begin discussing a possible mutual legal assistance treaty (MLAT) to facilitate the investigation and prosecution of many crimes, including terrorism, cyber crimes, and white collar offenses. They eventually signed a bilateral MLAT, Japan's first, in August 2003. At around the same time the two countries began bilateral talks on critical infrastructure protection, but progress was slow at first since both sides were in the process of revamping IT security organizations and policies. The United States and Japan did produce a joint statement in September 2003 on "promoting global cyber security," recognizing their "roles as global leaders to create a 'culture of security'...and highlight best practices in addressing cyber security issues and the importance of public-private partnerships in [implementation]." The statement encouraged the governments to work within appropriate multilateral forums, such as APEC, the G-8, and the OECD, to implement cyber security and cyber crime recommendations, and it endorsed the Council of Europe Convention on Cybercrime.[95]

Interestingly, the statement suggested that each government identify and empower a centralized authority to develop and coordinate national cyber security policies "in a holistic intergovernmental manner," but then proceeded to cloud the issue at the end of the document. The Cabinet Secretariat's IT Security Office is clearly identified as the centralized authority on the Japan side, and in the United States it is ostensibly the DHS's National Cyber Security Division. But the statement went on to say, perhaps for U.S. domestic, political-bureaucratic reasons, that the DHS "coordinates closely with the Department of State on international issues, which has the lead for U.S. foreign policy. The Department of Justice and the Federal Bureau of Investigation lead the national effort to investigate and prosecute cyber crime. The Homeland Security Council at the White House ensures coordination of all homeland security-related policy among federal and executive agencies." On top of this, the forum itself at which the statement was drafted was organized by the Department of Commerce's Office of Electronic Commerce. The instinct for offices and agencies to build fences around their portfolios, people, and budgets is understandable, but if the benefits of international cooperation are to be realized, then patterns of communication must be as clear and streamlined as possible.

On the multilateral side, a successful effort has been the G-8 Subgroup on High-Tech Crime, formed in 1997. One result was the establishment of a round-the-clock network of law enforcement points of contact for high-tech crime activities in each of the G-8 countries. A recent study noted that these kinds of multilateral efforts help identify key issues for governments and organizations to address, but that ultimately cooperation for a specific incident is largely carried out bilaterally between affected countries, suggesting that the multilateral approach often fosters bilateral cooperation rather than replaces it.[96] Japan is also working with Australia on an initiative within the APEC Telecommunications and Information Working group to help other members develop their own national computer emergency response capabilities. National watch, warning, and analysis centers are the first step in developing an international architecture for exchanging information on incidents on the Internet, a stated U.S. goal in its international outreach and cooperation efforts. In this respect, Japan and the United States are working toward the same goals internationally, but their efforts are not yet sufficiently coordinated to yield the maximum efficiencies.

With regard to bioterrorism, the 2001 anthrax attacks in the United States caused crisis managers in both countries to reevaluate their current policies and procedures for handling these types of problems. Although dealing with the effects of a bioterrorist attack is almost always a domestic activity, the international implications were quickly evident in 2001, as Japanese authorities responded to over one thousand anthrax-related hoaxes within two months after the first tainted letter appeared in the United States. The impact will be even more direct if bioterror involves attempts to spread epidemic diseases such as smallpox. At the law enforcement level, the anthrax attacks had the immediate effect of prompting Japan to revise its laws enabling the government to punish those who perpetrate acts of bioterrorism. The recently agreed-to MLAT mentioned above is also relevant to the issue. But the most promising avenue for cooperation probably lies in the areas of exchange (and in some cases co-development) of technologies and vaccines designed to sense and help respond to an incident. It is simply inefficient and too costly for each nation to develop and maintain its own vaccine stockpiles, and there might also be occasions when research into commercially non-viable technologies might be appropriately shared among developed countries. As in the case of cyber security, the United States and Japan can be leaders in a multilateral setting to help agree upon priorities in this area and on a plan for achieving them.[97] One such setting is APEC, where regional leaders in October 2003 welcomed the establishment, by Singapore and the United States, of the Regional Emerging Disease Intervention Centre, and agreed to other initiatives related to counter-terrorism in the health field.

Another resource that should not be overlooked with regard to bilateral or multilateral cooperation in this area is PACOM, given its links to other commands in the U.S. military with significant experience with biological defense issues that could be applied to a terrorist or missile attack in Japan involving biological weapons (BW). U.S. Central Command, for example, has conducted a number of studies and exercises related to BW defense and consequence management issues. NATO has also been looking at issues of detection, identification, early warning, medical capability and requirements, and post-attack restoration of operations.[98] PACOM could be a valuable resource for USFJ to engage Japan's SDF in studies and planning for possible scenarios that might involve their combined resources.

Notes for Chapter Four

55 The Global Partnership and Common Agenda were broad agreements between the United States and Japan to cooperate and pool resources when appropriate in efforts addressing certain region-

al and global problems such as environmental degradation, poverty, and disease.

56 Ashton B. Carter and William J. Perry, "Back to the Brink," *Washington Post,* October 20, 2002.

57 Jamie McIntyre, "Washington Was on the Brink of War with North Korea 5 Years Ago," *CNN.com,* October 4, 1999, http://www.cnn.com/US/9910/04/korea.brink/index.html.

58 Takashi Arimoto, Fumito Ishibashi, and Makiko Takita, "Keeping a Lock on Important Information…Fierce Battle," *Tokyo Sankei Shimbun,* August 19, 2003, part 3 of a three-part series entitled "Do Bureaucrats Reign Supreme? – Behind Political Leadership," FBIS document JPP20030819000047.

59 U.S. Department of Defense, Office of International Security Affairs, *United States Security Strategy for the East Asia-Pacific Region* (Washington, D.C., February 1995).

60 For the full text of the joint declaration, see *Federation of American Scientists News,* http://www.fas.org/news/Japan/11318448-11333165.htm.

61 The Defense Policy Review Initiative was launched at the U.S.-Japan Security Consultative Committee meeting on December 16, 2002. For the joint statement from that meeting, section 10, see *Japan Ministry of Foreign Affairs Official Web Site,* http://www.mofa.go.jp/region/n-america/us/security/scc/joint0212.html.

62 See Charles M. Perry and Toshi Yoshihara, *The U.S.-Japan Alliance: Preparing for Korean Reconciliation and Beyond* (Herndon, Virginia: Brassey's, 2003), in particular chapter 4.

63 Tomohito Shinoda, "Koizumi's Top-Down Leadership in the Anti-Terrorism Legislation: The Impact of Political Institution Changes," *SAIS Review* 23, no. 1 (winter-spring 2003): 19-34.

64 Ibid. The reforms of 1999 were the result of coalition government negotiations between the Liberal Democratic Party and the Liberal Party in January 1999, and led to a smaller (and presumably more unified) cabinet, among other changes.

65 This office includes a group in charge of IT security and policy toward post-war Iraq. There are three assistant chief cabinet secretaries (ACCS) overseeing this office and they generally come from the Defense Agency, the NPA, and MOFA. The assistant chief cabinet secretary from the Defense Agency assumes various responsibilities related to national security and crisis management, and he often works closely with the deputy chief cabinet secretary for crisis management (DCCS CM - usually from the NPA) and the DCCS for administration.

66 Leo Bosner, a U.S. Federal Emergency Management Agency disaster management expert who spent a year observing emergency

management structures and procedures in Japan as a Mansfield Fellow, notes that – among other problems – the Cabinet Office Disaster Management Bureau is still too small to manage the response to a major disaster. Compared to fifty in Japan, FEMA has a headquarters staff of about eight hundred and a national staff of over two thousand. Leo Bosner, "Emergency Management in Japan," manuscript obtained by editor (October 2001).

67 "Keeping a Lock on Important Information...Fierce Battle," *Tokyo Sankei Shimbun*, August 19, 2003.

68 Mari Yamaguchi, "Japan Extends Military's Right to Fight," Associated Press, June 6, 2003.

69 "Diet Enact Three National Emergency Bills," *Foreign Press Center/Japan*, June 13, 2003, http://www.fpcj.jp/e/shiryo/jb/0333.html.

70 Government of Japan, Ministry of Foreign Affairs, *Legislation on the Response in the Case of an Armed Attack and Other such Emergency and Japan's Foreign Policy* (Tokyo, June 2003).

71 See Perry and Yoshihara, *The U.S.-Japan Alliance*, 33-49, for a discussion of the evolution of Japanese perspectives on security and defense policies.

72 Ilene R. Prusher, "Tokyo Readies for the 'Big One,'" *Christian Science Monitor*, September 1, 2000.

73 "Disaster Drills Follow Tragedy," *Mainichi Shimbun*, September 1, 2001.

74 Exercises of this type are regularly scheduled for September 1, which is the anniversary of the 1923 Great Kanto Earthquake and is nationally observed as Disaster Preparedness Day.

75 "Enhancing U.S.-Japanese Cooperation on Crisis and Consequence Management," second IFPA/OSIPP workshop, Tokyo, Japan, April 10-11, 2002.

76 Japan Defense Agency, *Defense of Japan*, 2002, 127-28.

77 "SDF Peacekeeping Force Eyed by Defense Agency," *Japan Times*, July 16, 2003.

78 The Coral Sea exercise in September 2003 was the first of several planned under the Proliferation Security Initiative, which is designed to prevent the shipment of WMD or other illicit cargo. Japan, the United States, Australia, and seven other countries started the initiative. Japan's Coast Guard played a lead role in the exercise, which practiced intercepting a U.S. naval vessel pretending to be a freighter carrying chemical weapons.

79 "Enhancing U.S.-Japanese Cooperation on Crisis and Consequence Management," second IFPA/OSIPP workshop, Tokyo, Japan, April 10-11, 2002.

80 Robyn Pangi, "Consequence Management in the 1995 Sarin Attacks on the Japanese Subway System," BCSIA discussion paper

2002-4, ESDP discussion paper ESDP-2002-01 (John F. Kennedy School of Government, Harvard University, February 2002).

81　Ibid., 32.

82　The DHS and NORTHCOM are separate and not connected in any formal way, either in terms of decision making or budget formulation.

83　Many of the broad policies and objectives of the new DHS derive from the "National Strategy for Homeland Security," Office of Homeland Security (the White House, July 16, 2002).

84　As of October 2003, the office consisted of five people.

85　"Departments of State, Homeland Security Reach Agreement on Visa Oversight to Better Secure America's Borders," U.S. Department of Homeland Security press release, September 29, 2003.

86　The White House, "The National Security to Secure Cyberspace," February 2003. One recommendation, for example, is to work with Canada and Mexico to make North America a "safe cyber zone," which to the extent it deals with networks related to energy, water, and other physical systems makes sense. But the recommendation also includes banking, finance, and other global networks, which suggests that the inclusion of Japanese and Europeans, at least as observers, would be beneficial.

87　Michael Hirsh, "Bioterror: Stepping on Toes?" *Newsweek*, October 6, 2003.

88　The Unified Command Plan allocates responsibilities among the nine combatant commands. It establishes the commands' missions, responsibilities, and force structure. The plan also defines the geographical commands' areas of responsibilities. Before NORTH-COM, there was no single U.S. command dedicated to the defense of United States territory in the way that NORTHCOM is structured. NORTHCOM is headquartered in Peterson Air Force Base in Colorado, co-located with the North American Aerospace Defense Command (NORAD).

89　See Perry and Yoshihara, *The U.S.-Japan Alliance*, 8-33, for a discussion of the implications of America's global strategy for the Asia-Pacific region.

90　"PACAF's Air Operations Center Participates in Fuji-Yama Sakura," Pacific Air Forces News Service (PACAFNS), January 29, 2003.

91　Japan Defense White Paper, 2003, reference 29 (in Japanese).

92　"MSDF Put Sailors on U.S. Craft After 9/11," *Kyodo News* (Sasebo), September 15, 2003.

93　Kanako Takahara, "Panel Calls for Reinterpretation of the Antiwar Constitution," *Japan Times*, September 19, 2003.

94　The Northern Territories generally refers to four islands in the Kuril Island chain northeast of Hokkaido, seized by the Soviet Union in the waning days of World War II and claimed by both Russia and Japan (though controlled by the former). This territorial dispute has prevented Japan and Russia from signing a formal peace treaty since the end of the war.

95 U.S. Embassy, Tokyo, "United States – Japan Joint Statement on Promoting Global Cyber Security," September 9, 2003.

96 James A. Lewis, editor, *Cyber Security: Turning National Solutions into International Cooperation* (Washington, D.C.: Center for Strategic and International Studies, 2003), 4-5.

97 Much of this information regarding U.S.-Japan cooperation in bioterrorism was drawn from a unique conference co-organized by the Japan Society and the National Institute for Research Advancement in July 2002. See the conference report, "Bioterrorism and Consequence Management: New Approaches to U.S.-Japan Security Cooperation" (New York, Japan Society, Inc., 2003).

98 Operation Desert Breeze in the late 1990s was one of the largest and most comprehensive. See summary report and proceedings from "NATO and Biological Defense: Improving Allied Preparedness and Capabilities," NATO Headquarters, July 2000.

CHAPTER FIVE

Recommendations for Cooperation & Collaboration

✤

As outlined in the case studies and subsequent chapters of this study, there clearly exist opportunities for enhanced focus on crisis and consequence management in each country and for cooperative endeavors between the two. It is not enough, however, to make broad statements about the self-evident need for greater cooperation in the field of crisis management. Few would argue against the theoretical benefits of closer collaboration, but the reality is that time and money are limited. Crisis management cooperation between the United States and Japan competes with other bilateral priorities, and the crisis and consequence managers in both countries already have a full plate of pressing domestic needs to address.

The key to realizing the benefits of cooperation in this area, therefore, is to integrate crisis and consequence management into existing alliance structures, rather than add a new layer of issues to the agenda. As a part of this process, the two countries need to agree on a relatively small set of clear priorities that can supplement bilateral and multilateral work already taking place. Until recently, the military and political aspects of the alliance have largely progressed on two separate tracks, but the "track" analogy is increasingly becoming irrelevant. Instead, the military and political (even economic) tracks today seem more like lanes on a highway, divided for organizational purposes but easily crossed and influencing one another more directly. Responding to this development proactively could serve to enhance the alliance and prepare it for the challenges of the new century.

Basic Steps to Facilitate Cooperation

For good reason, the United States and Japan will first and foremost be focused on continuing to improve their own domestic crisis and consequence management capabilities. Each government's primary responsibility is to its citizens, and domestic preparedness is the most important mission for crisis managers. That said, at this critical stage in domestic reform, both nations have a unique opportunity to factor bilateral and multilateral cooperative aspects into their organizational and policy refinements. The following, then, are basic policy recommendations for each country to consider as it moves forward with domestic reform.

Japan

1. Continue working to improve crisis and consequence management capabilities (at the national and local levels), integrating emergency preparedness, response, recovery, and prevention, and possibly including consideration of establishing a national emergency management agency.
2. Continue clarifying and codifying the details regarding national emergency legislation, particularly with regard to interaction with USFJ.
3. Follow through on proposed plans to strengthen the Security Council of Japan so that it can play an advisory and consultative role to the prime minister with full-time staff drawn from other ministries.
4. Identify one position or office (either in a strengthened Security Council or in the Cabinet Secretariat) that can be a primary point of contact or coordinator for U.S.-Japan crisis and consequence management co-

      operation, drawing on the work of other ministries and agencies.

5. In coordination with the primary point of contact recommended above, explore the establishment of a special committee or task force within the Japanese Federation of Economic Organizations (Nippon Keidanren) to be a liaison between the Japanese business community and government on these issues.

6. Increase the number of staff at the Disaster Management Bureau within the Cabinet Office (or at least design and practice arrangements for quickly ramping up the bureau's size and capabilities during a crisis).[99]

7. Continue steps to better integrate the SDF in national and local crisis/consequence management planning (including theater missile defense capabilities), keeping in mind opportunities to take advantage of USFJ assets.

8. Factor crisis and consequence management issues into DPRI discussions with the United States and as part of Japan's National Defense Program Outline revisions due in 2004.

9. Continue carrying out crisis and consequence management drills and exercises with an emphasis on pushing decision making and logistical capabilities to the breaking point.

10. Strengthen domestic laws governing the protection of classified information to facilitate ever more open exchange of intelligence among allies.

11. Pursue a policy of clarifying Japan's ability to exercise its right of collective self-defense, as allowed for in the UN charter, in a legal and transparent manner that is reassuring to other nations in the region.

United States

1. Continue with the establishment and refinement of the DHS with a focus on efficient sharing of information among departments and clarifying bureaucratic responsibility and accountability.

2. As DHS evolves, avoid papering over differences between agencies and departments that stem from bureaucratic history or tradition and instead foster a culture of common purpose, common understanding, and common action.

3. Pay particular attention to the triangular relationship of DHS, DoD, and the State Department, recognizing the critical role this plays in interacting with allies and the problems that can be caused by poor communication and disconnected initiatives.

4. Consider explicitly identifying an office at the American Embassy in Tokyo (perhaps the deputy chief of mission) as a primary point of contact or coordinator for U.S.-Japan crisis and consequence management cooperation, drawing on the work of other departments and agencies (as a counterpart to the suggested position in recommendation 4 for Japan, above), and also developing good relations with Japan's DCCS CM and DCCS Admin.

5. In coordination with a primary point of contact at the American Embassy, explore the establishment of a special committee or task force at the American Chamber of Commerce in Japan (ACCJ) to be a liaison between the U.S. business community and government on these issues.

6. Seek to extend the U.S. perimeter of preparedness by working actively with allies and international organizations, avoiding an island mentality that tends to believe domestic crisis and consequence management preparation ends at North America's borders.

7. Increase the number of staff at DHS and the State Department specifically charged with facilitating international cooperation on certain crisis and consequence management issues.

8. Factor crisis and consequence management issues into DPRI discussions with Japan and follow through on recommendations to incorporate crisis and con-

sequence management scenarios in BCM planning exercises.

9. Conduct more regular and larger-scale crisis and consequence management drills that occasionally involve the public at large.

All of these steps are essentially aimed at improving domestic preparedness, though in some situations international cooperation is a supplemental means toward that end. In the U.S.-Japan case, collaboration is also a way for the two countries to take advantage of the trend of convergence that is occurring, in terms of converging interests, converging approaches to crisis management, and the converging security, political, and economic aspects of the bilateral relationship. To be sure, the United States and Japan still have their differences, whether over policy (such as trade or certain foreign policies) or in cultural, legal, and organizational behavior. The two countries' interests and approaches will never completely meet, but the overall trend is toward closer alignment, given their political, economic, and demographic foundations and global technological development. Because managing cooperation for any one aspect of the relationship in an environment of aligning interest and approach is relatively straightforward, there is reason to expect that U.S.-Japan performance on this front will continue to improve over time. The convergence of multiple aspects of the relationship (the heretofore separate security, political, and economic tracks, or lanes), however, presents a different challenge for the alliance. Managing this development efficiently will require leadership from both countries and possibly some adjustments to the way each nation shares information and responsibility within (and between) its civilian and military organizations. Interagency cooperation is increasingly vital for the alliance to achieve its full potential.

The "One-Two-Three" Approach

To help U.S. and Japanese policy makers take advantage of the crisis and consequence management opportunities that accompany the dramatic change going on in both countries, the project organizers have developed a "one-two-three" approach that could help facilitate cooperation and maximize its benefits. This approach is a simple way to express how the United States and Japan might go about building a shared framework for enhancing crisis and consequence management cooperation for both countries' advantage, including and beyond the basic steps outlined above.

The one-two-three approach begins with each nation identifying *one* primary point of contact or coordinator for crisis and consequence management issues (alluded to in recommendation 4, above, for each country). It continues with a focus on *two* categories of primary targets or priorities for cooperation (bilateral and multilateral), and on *three* methods of cooperation (exchanges, exercises, and strategic planning). This approach could be useful in helping the allies keep track of how they cooperate and making sure that each agency or department understands how its activities relate to a larger scheme of cooperative efforts. The key to successful implementation of this approach is that it should involve the least necessary bureaucratic coordination or imposition of a top-down hierarchy. Cooperation in the field of crisis and consequence management is, by its nature, diverse and involves many different scenarios and actors. It does not need to be tightly controlled, but rather it can be more effectively coordinated and implemented.

One: Crisis/Consequence Traffic Manager for the Alliance Roadway

Before discussing precisely what the alliance should focus on in the area of crisis and consequence management cooperation, it is worthwhile considering how these priorities might be addressed within existing alliance management structures. The simplest approach would be for each country to explicitly identify one primary point of contact or coordinator for U.S.-Japan crisis and consequence management cooperation, drawing on the work of the other departments and ministries. For the United States, the American Embassy in Tokyo could easily serve as the primary nexus for this aspect of bilateral cooperation, given its central role in any crisis involving the two countries. In many respects the embassy is already performing this function, but the effort is diffused across many issues and departments. The embassy has direct links to all the major components of the relationship, to the U.S. president via a well-connected and respected ambassador, to the secretary of state (and the secretary of defense by connection to the Japan-U.S. Security Consultative Committee, or 2+2), to USFJ and the Joint Coordination Group, to other relevant U.S. departments with staff serving at the embassy, and even to the legislative branch via visiting members of Congress, not to mention the close contacts with the Japanese central and regional governments.

The deputy chief of mission at the embassy currently plays the role of policy traffic manager for the entire spectrum of bilateral issues, but there is no one person with a specific portfolio that links commerce, customs, security, foreign policy, overseas aid, science and technology, treasury, and other policy areas in the context of crisis and consequence management. This results in a less than ideal exchange of information and clarity of purpose that relies on personal and bureaucratic relationships, which ebb and flow depending on who is serving in various key positions at any given time. Although the embassy already operates under an extremely tight budget relative to its responsibilities, the addition of one special assistant to the deputy chief of mission for crisis and consequence management could pay valuable dividends for the United States. This position would help bridge the gaps that currently exist between departments and between domestic and international efforts in this field. It would also be a simple way for the United States and Japan to communicate and cooperate with regard to preparedness and in times of crisis.

An additional idea to supplement a government point of contact is to encourage the American business community to create a similar position so that views from the private sector can be incorporated into official discussions of crisis and consequence management policies and cooperation. The ACCJ would be an ideal candidate to act as this point of contact. The ACCJ (with nearly thirty-two hundred members from over thirteen hundred companies) has created about sixty committees to help promote commerce between the two countries, exchange information, and promote the interests of its members. Its committees include air cargo, the travel industry, transportation and logistics, telecommunications, e-business, government relations, banking and finance, pharmaceuticals, and other issue areas related to the tasks at hand. Adding a small committee dedicated to harnessing the talents and activities of the chamber in support of governments' efforts with regard to crisis and consequence management could be an efficient way to involve the private sector.

On the Japan side of the equation, a similar structure can be established relatively easily. The most likely counterpart to the U.S. deputy chief of mission's assistant would either be someone directly assisting the DCCS CM or someone within the ACCS offices. If Japan does go forward to strengthen the Security Council with a larger support staff to provide advisory and consultative functions, it might also be possible to insert the point of contact there. The important issue is that the position should be placed at a convenient intersecting point of the Defense Agency, MOFA, and the wider cabinet organization. To mirror the role of a special ACCJ committee focused on crisis and consequence management cooperation issues, a similar committee could be established at Japan's premier business lobby, Nippon Keidanren. These simple adjustments would go a long way to helping the United States and Japan achieve their goals for cooperation in this area.

Two: Categories of Priority Targets

The next question to address is what ought to be the allies' goals or targets for cooperation. Given the universal limitations of time and money, it is useful for the United States and Japan to agree on a relatively small set of priorities for cooperation and collaboration. These priorities can be divided into two broad categories of bilateral and multilateral initiatives.

On the bilateral front, an obvious goal is to coordinate preparations and consequence management scenarios for certain catastrophic events that could occur in Japan, such as a massive earthquake (on the scale of Kobe or larger) or a nuclear accident, where USFJ assets or U.S. domestic expertise can effectively support the Japanese response. In the process of cooperating in this area, the two countries are likely to identify lessons or certain Japanese capabilities that could aid American planners for their own domestic preparations. A report in September 2003 by Japan's Central Disaster Management Council indicated that a worst-case scenario could involve three simultaneous earthquakes in three separate areas of Japan, which apparently did happen in 1707 and 1854. The report estimated that such an event could kill up to thirty thousand people and cause over $700 billion worth of damage.[100] If anything near such a disaster were to strike Japan, it would behoove the government to take advantage of all the resources at its disposal, including the U.S.-Japan alliance. This kind of cooperation would benefit the United States as well, for reasons described earlier in the study (including service to American citizens and businesses in Japan, protecting USFJ assets and capabilities, and demonstrating the tangible value of the alliance to the Japanese people, beyond relatively unlikely domestic war scenarios). Yet another aspect of this exercise could include bilateral cooperation in support of a joint response to similar disasters in other, poorer countries in the region.

An additional bilateral contingency for which the allies can consider planning is a missile attack by North Korea on Japan, particularly one that involves a chemical or nuclear weapon. The important difference in planning for this type of scenario is that it would likely entail both crisis and consequence management functions, including intelligence sharing, quick diplomatic decision making, deploying untested technologies, and a timely coordinated crisis and consequence response after the fact. Lessons learned through a focus on this priority should also be applicable to certain, broader terrorist-based threats, such as regional hijackings (of an oil tanker, cruise ship, or airline), bioterrorism, or proliferation of WMD. These latter threats are examples of issues that begin to cross the bilateral-multilateral line, but cooperation on preparing for and countering these threats will retain some purely bilateral components.

Multilateral cooperation on many of these issues is already being pursued by the United States and Japan, and these efforts should continue with strong American and Japanese leadership. Countering terrorism, responding to regional disasters or incidents, and preparing for disruptions to cyber and energy security are all tasks that can only be dealt with comprehensively in a multilateral setting. Multilateral bodies cannot make bold achievements in a short time frame unless there is a clear consensus as to the nature of a particular problem, the overall objective, and a short list of possible means to reach the desired goal. This kind of consensus is rare, however, so patience and diligence are required to be successful in these forums.

Priorities in the multilateral arena are already emerging, and a recent action plan agreed to at an APEC meeting in October 2003 touches on many of them. The plan ostensibly focuses on countering terrorism, and it addresses enhancing secure trade, halting terrorist financing, and promoting cyber security, energy security, and the health of communities.[101] This is an appropriate short list from which U.S.-Japan cooperation on multilateral initiatives can begin, but there is no need for the issues to be seen only through a lens of countering terrorism or for limiting discussion to APEC. Oil spills, nuclear waste issues, controlling epidemic diseases, and other non-terrorist-related challenges can also be discussed in this context. The United Nations and its related agencies, the European Union, the G-8, and others will also be involved, so it is clear that the United States and Japan will need to coordinate effectively with other allies to achieve progress on this front. Independent action by the allies in smaller, regional bodies is also a part of this process, but here again communication and collaboration between the two countries are important so that actions taken independently of each other are not redundant or do not run at cross purposes.[102]

Three: Methods of Cooperation

With an agreed-upon short list of priorities in hand, the allies must then decide how best to direct an appropriate amount of collaborative effort and resources in support of their objectives. The United States and Japan can, and should, continue to cooperate in bilateral and multilateral forums in three basic ways. The first is through information exchanges, which involve an organized and concerted effort to understand each other's capabilities, laws, procedures, and lessons learned as each pursues its own governmental and societal effort to plan for and help prevent crises. The second set of efforts should be planning and exercising to assist in certain situations drawn from the priorities identified above. Finally, and overarching this cooperation on the ground, the United States and Japan should conduct regular, strategic planning discussions at a relatively high level on these issues to continually shape the agenda, monitor progress, and coordinate strategy on the multilateral front. Specific recommendations, and the rationale for pursuing them, are broken out in these three broad categories below.

Information Exchanges and Lessons Learned

As mundane as it may sound, the United States and Japan need to update one another regularly on their legislation, policies, procedures, and institutional structures for crisis and consequence management. As has been shown in this study, each is undergoing significant changes in these areas, and in order for cooperation to take place, each must have a detailed and current knowledge of how the other is organized to address these challenges. While the law and organization are in place, the new DHS in the United States is likely to take several years to sort out its relationships and responsibilities within the U.S. government. On the international side, its relationship with the State Department, the DoD, and the intelligence communities – while set out formally in law and policy – will have to develop into a set of everyday actions and responsibilities.

There is no need to wait for the DHS dust to settle before the two countries begin formal exchanges and initiatives. Even though the DHS is understandably stretched thin in terms of budget and manpower, proactive international engagement (coordinated with the State Department) is a vital component of fulfilling the department's domestic mission. Personnel exchanges and long-term relationships should be established between the DHS and appropriate counterpart ministries and agencies within the Japanese government, in addition to current programs involving the State Department and other U.S. government agencies with Japan. Long-term exchanges, such as the Mansfield Fellowship Program, should be expanded and enhanced to ensure that a range of DHS employees travel and work in Japan and that a reciprocal program is created for Japanese crisis managers.[103] Shorter-term briefings and exchanges will also be useful.

An additional next step is for the two sides to engage in reciprocal understanding of both past crises and current exercises regarding crisis and consequence management. Both Japan and the United States are cultures that study and analyze history extensively. In the disaster prevention and disaster response communities in both countries, there is a strong cultural predisposition to studying past incidents for lessons. The military communities in each country also have a strong planning and review culture. The disaster response community does cooperate and share information across borders to some extent, but this inclination needs to be more systematized and widened to include the broader crisis and consequence management communities, including the military. Enhanced and systematized case study analysis, conducted by joint teams, would bring unique perspectives to the studies and allow different experiences and understandings to be brought to bear. While this research project consisted of Japanese teams primarily studying cases of accidents and incidents in Japan and American teams studying cases that occurred in the United States, a joint approach – or even one that consciously reverses the roles – could be undertaken both at the academic and government levels. Involving foreign observers in domestic exercises should always be considered, though there will of course be times when foreign involvement is either inconvenient or unnecessary.

In areas where the private sector – either the medical community or the business community with its reliance on cyberspace – conducts exercises and simulations, a system of sharing information should be developed as well. Here the ACCJ-Nippon

Keidanren relationship could play an important role. The medical community, through the normal system of academic publishing and conferences, does exchange data and information on such issues as medical responses to and treatments for chemical, biological, and radiological incidents and attacks. A more routinized system of exchanges should be established, however, perhaps building on the worldwide cooperation that has evolved out of the SARS epidemic. In cyber security, sharing of lessons learned is more difficult given reluctance on the part of businesses to reveal potential vulnerabilities that may have fiscal consequences. Still, sector-level initiatives, working through the industry-run ISACs, may be the place to begin such exchanges on an international level, perhaps first involving those companies with substantial operations in both countries. Additional points are listed below:

- Exchanges will continue to percolate up from the lower levels of bureaucracy, as needs or opportunities are identified, but senior policy makers (using the crisis/consequence traffic manager concept described above) can increasingly articulate broader goals and strategies.

- Information exchanges should be steered toward a more formalized, regularized, and comprehensive format (to include state/prefecture and local as well as national-level information).

- Exchanges should not be managed by a central authority, but the single point of contact or coordinator should be informed of all cooperative activities so that appropriate information can be disseminated to other offices and to inform the planning activities and strategic discussions.

- The United States could adopt Japan's national drills/exercise day concept, and Japan could learn from U.S. methods for better inter-ministerial communication and better national-local collaboration and communication. This is a good area for information exchange.

- Where possible, each government should implement information exchanges with universities and the private sector. Information should flow back and forth between government and the general public as much as possible in this area, to take advantage of emerging technologies and achievements in basic science, and to foster a cross-fertilization of ideas and approaches.

• Capabilities rosters, with timelines, could be assembled and exchanged for a variety of contingencies that could occur in the United States, Japan, or a third country in the East Asia region.

• The allies should increase and regularize intelligence exchange on potential and pending threats in third countries as the basis for joint planning and exercises, where possible.

Planning and Exercising to Assist

While Japan has shown its solidarity and support in crises such as September 11 and operation Enduring Freedom, it is more likely – given the presence of U.S. bases and military forces in Japan – that it will be the United States rendering direct assistance in Japan or in the region during a future crisis.[104] As discussed earlier, Japan has significant resources and expertise on which it can rely when needed, so most emergencies will easily be handled by Japan alone. It is only in cases of very large-scale natural disasters, accidents, or uniquely troubling events as outlined above when U.S. assets might lend support to Japan's own crisis and consequence management operation. In addition, accidents or incidents involving U.S. bases in Japan are also an important contingency. Planning and exercising to assist one another is a relatively straightforward method of communication. Some points for consideration are listed below:

• The United States and Japan should increase the scope and frequency of joint, national-level (with local involvement) drills and exercises on a range of crisis/consequence management events, including WMD incidents and counter-terrorism efforts.

• Exercises should emphasize efficient and effective information flow across bureaucratic organizations and between countries in addition to testing physical responses and preparations.

- Exercises should include a prominent public affairs component wherever possible.
- Involvement of SDF in recent disaster drills was significant; USFJ involvement (with reachback to PACOM) can begin at tabletop/command post exercise level and grow to a field training exercise so as to minimize inconveniences to the public.
- U.S. and Japanese reciprocal reviews of plans, and participation as designers and controllers in each other's exercises (in certain cases), would help each to understand assumptions better and to provide input on where and when important issues are not being addressed.
- The United States and Japan should undertake or encourage, where viable, joint research and development on technologies required for crisis/consequence management, such as NBC weapons detectors and quick-analysis capabilities, protective gear, medical responses and training, vaccine development, and intruder detection capabilities for cyber attacks.
- The United States and Japan should continue planning and exercises for joint responses to disasters and crises at sea or in third countries in the region.
- The United States and Japan should involve non-military players in military-related planning and exercises whenever possible, for example from other ministries with applicable capabilities, international organizations, or even non-governmental organizations.

Strategic Planning Discussions

Conducting regular, high-level policy discussions specifically focused on these issues is fundamentally different from the information exchanges described above, and these talks would essentially guide the overall process of cooperation. In designing and arranging the policy discussions, government officials need not create a new initiative of stand-alone dialogue, as in past initiatives regarding trade, deregulation, or even defense cooperation. While the Clinton-era Common Agenda can point to many successes, there were also shortcomings that should be taken into consideration. Specifically, there were complaints from a few offices that certain joint projects were created ahead of bilateral meetings more to demonstrate progress in the initiative than because they were particularly well designed or addressed a high priority. In addition, there are times when staff in charge of an initiative like the Common Agenda will try to co-opt successful projects in other jurisdictions and as a result create a negative, competitive atmosphere between agencies.

In this case we are not recommending a new crisis management initiative or a new layer of bureaucracy, but instead something along the lines of adding a specific agenda item on crisis and consequence management issues, perhaps as part of the 2+2 meetings linking each country's foreign policy and defense leaders, that would allow for regular, high-level briefings and discussions on policy directions and priorities. Top officials in both countries must stay involved in the overall process, not only to help provide strategic direction, but also to protect budgetary resources and inject a modicum of executive accountability.

From Awkward Movement to Flowing Mainstream

Despite the long and close relationship between the United States and Japan, the two countries are only just beginning to cooperate concretely in the field of crisis and consequence management. Recent progress has been significant, but in many ways both nations still interact awkwardly with each other, similar to how two dance partners might behave in the early days of practicing a new performance. This awkwardness is due not only to the fact that some of the issues are new to each side, but also because they are working with relatively new and untested bureaucratic tools to accomplish their tasks. The awkward moments will pass, however, as long as the two governments remain focused on and dedicated to improving and expanding communication, capabilities, and interoperability. Revising the Defense Guidelines took several years of negotiation, assimilation, explanation, debates on new legislation, and finally planning and practicing actual implementation. The benefits of that process, however, are clear to both countries, and each recognizes the contributions those revisions make to its own security. Other countries in the region have also derived benefits from a stable and well-functioning U.S.-Japan alliance.

The task that lies before U.S. and Japanese leaders is not nearly as complicated and politically sensitive as the Defense Guidelines revision issue was when it was first discussed in the mid-1990s, but bringing crisis and consequence management functions into the mainstream of existing alliance dialogues and activities will still be a significant challenge. The most difficult aspect of the challenge will probably be how to achieve the goal in a simple and efficient manner, without occupying too much time and expense, or demanding too much attention from the two nations' top leaders. It is unlikely that President Bush and Prime Minister Koizumi would issue a grand declaration on bilateral crisis management cooperation, nor should one be necessary or advised. It is also true, however, that simply allowing current trends to continue will not result in a satisfactory level of cooperation, and doing so could represent an important opportunity missed. Pulling together the existing threads of various crisis and consequence management initiatives (bilateral and multilateral) and weaving them, together with new undertakings, into a more productive pattern of cooperation will require effort and leadership, but it is entirely achievable and desirable. The U.S.-Japan alliance will be stronger for it, and so will be the prospects for greater global stability and cohesion.

Notes for Chapter Five

99 This recommendation would not be necessary if Japan did indeed decide to establish a national emergency management agency.

100 Peggy Hernandez, "Japanese Specialists Tremble at the Specter of a New Big One," *Boston Globe*, October 12, 2003.

101 See "Countering Terrorism Action Plan: Combined Report from APEC Fora," submitted by the APEC Secretariat for the Conclud-

ing Senior Officials' Meeting in Bangkok, Thailand, October 14-15, 2003.

102 Examples of independent involvement in multilateral efforts include a one-day meeting in Tokyo in September 2003 for crisis managers from nine Asian cities to discuss measures against terrorist attacks made with NBC weapons and Japan's cooperation with ASEAN in regional efforts to monitor and contain SARS.

103 Information on the Mansfield Fellowship Program can be found at *The Maureen and Mike Mansfield Foundation*, http://www. mansfieldfdn.org/fellow/fellow.htm. Over sixty U.S. government officials have participated in the program since it began in 1995, many of whom now serve in positions at the American Embassy in Tokyo, Treasury Department, Justice Department, FEMA, DoD, Energy Department, Commerce Department, Health and Human Services Department, and the military services.

104 That is, unless a regional event requires a military response for which Japan is unable to take the lead, in which case the roles will be reversed.

List of Abbreviations

⌗

2+2	Refers to the Japan-U.S. Security Consultative Committee meetings
ACCJ	American Chamber of Commerce in Japan
ACCS	Assistant chief cabinet secretary (Japan)
APEC	Asia Pacific Economic Cooperation
ASEAN	Association of Southeast Asian Nations
BCC	Bilateral coordination center
BCM	Bilateral coordination mechanism
BW	Biological weapons
CBP	Customs and Border Protection (United States)
CBRN	Chemical, biological, radiological, and nuclear
CDPC	Central Disaster Prevention Council (Japan)
CERT	Computer emergency response team
CIAO	Critical Infrastructure Assurance Office (United States)
DCCS-Admin	Deputy chief cabinet secretary for administration (Japan)
DCCS CM	Deputy chief cabinet secretary for crisis management (Japan)
DDOS	Distributed denial of service
DHS	Department of Homeland Security (United States)
DoD	Department of Defense (United States)
DPRI	Defense Policy Review Initiative (United States and Japan)
FBI	Federal Bureau of Investigation (United States)
FEMA	Federal Emergency Management Agency (United States)
GWOT	Global war on terrorism
HDC	Headquarters for Disaster Countermeasures (Japan)
HHS	Department of Health and Human Services (United States)

135

IAEA	International Atomic Energy Agency
IFPA	Institute for Foreign Policy Analysis
ISAC	Information sharing and analysis center
IT	Information technology
JCO	Japan Nuclear Fuel Conversion Company
Nippon Keidanren	Japanese Federation of Economic Organizations
LDP	Liberal Democratic Party (Japan)
METI	Ministry of Economy, Trade and Industry (Japan)
MLAT	Mutual legal assistance treaty
MOFA	Ministry of Foreign Affairs (Japan)
MPT	Ministry of Posts and Telecommunications (Japan)
NBC	Nuclear, biological, or chemical
NGO	Non-governmental organization
NIPC	National Infrastructure Protection Center (United States)
NIRS	National Institute of Radiological Sciences (Japan)
NISA	Nuclear and Industrial Safety Agency (Japan)
NORTHCOM	U.S. Northern Command
NPA	National Police Agency (Japan)
NPT	Nuclear Non-Proliferation Treaty
OECD	Organization for Economic Cooperation and Development
OSIPP	Osaka School of International Public Policy
PACOM	U.S. Pacific Command
PDD	Presidential decision directive (United States)
PSIA	Public Security Investigation Agency (Japan)
ROK	Republic of Korea
SARS	Severe acute respiratory syndrome
SDF	(Japanese) Self-Defense Forces
SOFA	Status of forces agreement
STA	Science and Technology Agency (Japan)
UN	United Nations
USFJ	U.S. Forces Japan
WMD	Weapons of mass destruction
Y2K	Year 2000

About the Contributors

Toshiya Hoshino is a professor of international security studies at Osaka University's School of International Public Policy. Professor Hoshino graduated from Sophia University and obtained an M.A. in international relations in 1986 from the University of Tokyo, and a Ph.D. from Osaka University. He was a political analyst at the Japanese Embassy in Washington, D.C., from 1998 to 1991 and a visiting fellow at the Woodrow Wilson School at Princeton University from 1992 to 1993. He also served as a senior research fellow at the Japan Institute of International Affairs until 1998. Professor Hoshino's recent publications include a chapter in *Containing Conflict: Cases in Preventive Diplomacy* (Japan Center for International Exchange, 2003); *Jindo-kiki to Kokusai Kainyu: Heiwa-kaifuku no Shohosen* [Humanitarian crises and international intervention: prescriptions for peace restoration] (co-authored in Japanese, Yushindo, 2003), and *Kokusai Kiki-gaku: Kiki Kanri to Yobo Gaiko* [International crisis studies: Crisis management and preventive diplomacy] (co-authored, Sekai Shiso Sha, 2002).

Dr. Charles M. Perry is vice president and director of studies at the Institute for Foreign Policy Analysis. He has written extensively on a variety of national and international security issues, especially with respect to defense trends and security policy in the Asia-Pacific region, NATO affairs and European security, arms trade and technology transfer problems, WMD proliferation concerns, missile defense options, and regional conflict issues. Principal areas of current research and analysis focus on U.S.-allied cooperation on crisis/consequence management, strategic developments and alliance adjustments in Northeast Asia, and challenges to regional stability along NATO's flanks, especially in the Nordic-Baltic and Balkan regions. Recent publications include *The U.S.-Japan Alliance: Preparing for Korean Reconciliation and Beyond* (Brassey's, 2003); *Defense Reform and Modernization in Southeast Europe* (IFPA, 2002); and *Strategic Dynamics in the Nordic-Baltic Region: Implications for U.S. Policy* (Brassey's, 2000). Dr. Perry holds an M.A. in international affairs, M.A. in law and diplomacy, and a Ph.D. in international politics from The Fletcher School of Law and Diplomacy, Tufts University.

James L. Schoff is a senior staff member at the Institute for Foreign Policy Analysis. He joined IFPA after serving as the program officer in charge of policy studies at the United States - Japan Foundation for nearly four years. Mr. Schoff specializes in American foreign policy and East Asian economic and security issues. Before working at the foundation, he spent five years (three based in Tokyo) developing new business and managing building projects (including an emergency housing project following the Kobe earthquake) in Asia for Bovis Construction, an international construction and project management firm. Prior to his work at Bovis, he assisted with foreign policy studies at the Brookings Institution. His recent publications include *The 108th Congress: Asia Pacific Policy Outlook* (National Bureau of Asian Research, 2003) and *WMD Challenges on the Korean Peninsula and New Approaches* (IFPA Conference Report, 2003). Mr. Schoff graduated from Duke University and earned an M.A. in international relations at the Johns Hopkins University School for Advanced International Studies (SAIS).

The *Osaka School of International Public Policy* (OSIPP) is a leading graduate program of Osaka University. OSIPP provides cutting-edge, multidisciplinary education and research in the fields of law, politics, and economics. The school offers a comprehensive educational and research program aimed at training professionals in the formulation of national and international public policy. OSIPP publishes a semi-annual journal containing articles authored by staff members and doctoral students in Japanese and English.

The Institute for Foreign Policy Analysis (IFPA) is an independent, non-partisan, and not-for-profit (501(c)(3)) research organization that conducts research, publishes studies, convenes seminars and conferences, promotes education, and trains policy analysts in the fields of foreign policy and national security affairs. The institute maintains a staff of specialists at its offices in Cambridge, Massachusetts, and Washington, D.C. IFPA is associated with The Fletcher School of Law and Diplomacy, Tufts University. Since its founding in 1976, IFPA has provided a forum for the examination of political, economic, security, and defense-industrial issues confronting the United States in a rapidly changing world.

Agenda
First IFPA-OSIPP Workshop

Enhancing U.S.-Japanese Cooperation on Crisis & Consequence Management

The Madison Hotel, Washington, D.C.

Wednesday, November 29, 2000

WELCOME AND INTRODUCTION

Professor Mitsuru Kurosawa, former Dean, OSIPP, Osaka University

Dr. Charles M. Perry, Vice President, IFPA

SESSION 1

Organizing for Crisis and Consequence Management: U.S. and Japanese Definitions, Procedures, and Operational Concepts

This session reviewed and summarized the basic approaches that the United States and Japan take, respectively, in preparing for, responding to, and managing the consequences of diverse crises, be they accidental or deliberate in origin. The goal was to improve both nations' understanding of how the other operates as a necessary basis for more effective collaboration. Topics of discussion and presentation included:

- How does each nation define and conceptualize crisis and consequence management?

- How does this affect the way(s) in which each nation organizes for the task(s) entailed?
- Operationally, who's in charge and does it vary from situation to situation? If so, how?
- What, more specifically, happens when nuclear, biological, chemical, and/or radiological (NBCR) agents or weapons are involved?
- How can proper coordination between military and non-military assets be assured?
- What is the current status of U.S.-Japanese crisis and consequence management cooperation? What mechanisms, procedures, negotiations, and agreements (if any) are in place?

Presentations

Overview of U.S. Approach to Establishing Consequence Management Requirements

Ms. Lisa Gordon-Hagerty, Director, Transnational Threats, National Security Council, The White House

U.S. Government's Response to WMD Terrorism

Mr. Sam Brinkley, Office of the Coordinator for Counterterrorism, Department of State

Japanese Approaches to Crisis Management

Professor Toshiya Hoshino, Osaka University.

Open discussion

SESSION 2

Lessons Learned from Recent Crises and Crisis Prevention Efforts

This session provided an opportunity for in-depth discussion of lessons learned across a variety of recent and/or likely crises regarding local-state-national coordination, interagency cooperation, capability gaps, civil-military collaboration, public relations strategy, and preventative measures.

Speakers

Mr. Richard Owens, Disaster Operations Specialist, Office of Foreign Disaster Assistance, USAID; **Ms. Lisa Weldon**, Planning and

Coordination Branch, Operations and Planning Division, Response and Recovery Directorate, FEMA; **Mr. H.K. Park**, Office of the Assistant to Secretary of Defense for Civil Support; **Dr. Shingo Nagamatsu**, Research Associate, Osaka School of International Public Policy

- Responding to Natural Disasters (e.g., Japanese experiences in Hanshin earthquake, U.S. experiences in providing overseas earthquake assistance, e.g., in Turkey and Taiwan, etc.)
- Responding to an NBCR Incident (e.g., Japanese experiences re: the 1995 Tokyo subway sarin attack and the 1999 Tokaimura accident; U.S. experiences re: WMD counter-terrorism and consequence management planning, etc.)

Open Discussion

Speakers

Captain Harlan Henderson, U.S. Coast Guard; **Mr. Paul Kurtz**, Director, Security, Infrastructure Protection, and Counterterrorism, U.S. National Security Council; **Dr. Hitoshi Okada**, Associate Professor, Human and Social Information Research, National Institute of Informatics

- Responding to Incidents at Sea (e.g., Japanese and U.S. Coast Guard experiences in handling oil/chemical spills; USCG plans in the WMD response arena, etc.)
- Coping with Cyber-warfare Threats (e.g., Japanese experiences in coping with recent cyber attacks, U.S. and Japanese planning to counter cyber-warfare)

Open Discussion

SESSION 3

**Options and Implications for
U.S.-Japanese Collaboration**

Drawing on discussions held in the first two sessions, the final segment served essentially as a brainstorming session, aimed at identifying the broad implications of past experiences and current policy planning for future U.S.-Japanese cooperation.

Speakers

RADM Donald Weiss, USN, Director of Asian and Pacific Affairs, OSD/ISA/AP; *Maj. Gen. Noboru Yamaguchi,* Japan Ground Self-Defense Force, Defense/Military Attaché, Embassy of Japan

- How might national differences identified above affect the prospects for – as well as the organization and effectiveness of – joint operations?
- Is there value in considering additional bilateral agreements and memoranda of understanding (MOUs) to facilitate U.S.-Japanese cooperation?
- What joint efforts/strategies can be undertaken to help prevent situations from evolving into crises?
- In the capabilities realm, where are the best opportunities for collaboration? Are they in R&D? Training and exercises? Greater transparency overall?
- What issues/areas could benefit most from further study?

Open Discussion

Particpants
First IFPA-OSIPP Workshop

JAPAN

Dr. Toshiya Hoshino, Associate Professor, International Politics and Security, Osaka School of International Public Policy, Osaka University

Mr. Masaki Ikegami, Assistant Director, Japan-U.S. Security Treaty Division, North American Affairs Bureau, Ministry of Foreign Affairs

Mr. Takashi Kawakami, Professor and Senior Research Fellow, National Institute for Defense Studies, Japan Defense Agency

Dr. Mitsuru Kurosawa, Professor and former Dean, Osaka School of International Public Policy, Osaka University

Dr. Shingo Nagamatsu, Research Associate, International Politics and Security, Osaka School of International Public Policy, Osaka University

Dr. Hitoshi Okada, Associate Professor, Human and Social Information Research, National Institute of Informatics

Maj. Gen. Noboru Yamaguchi, Japan Ground Self-Defense Force, Defense/Military Attaché, Embassy of Japan

THE UNITED STATES

Ms. Rachel Billingslea, Office of Plans and Counterproliferation, Office of the Assistant Secretary of Defense, Strategy and Threat Reduction, Office of the Secretary of Defense

Mr. Kevin Bratsch, Foreign Affairs Assistant, Consequence Management Program, Office of International Security Operations, Bureau of Political-Military Affairs, Department of State

Mr. Sam Brinkley, Special Advisor for WMD, Office of the Coordinator for Counterterrorism, Department of State

Dr. Thomas Cynkin, Special Assistant to the Deputy Secretary, Department of State

Dr. Jacquelyn K. Davis, Executive Vice President, Institute for Foreign Policy Analysis (IFPA)

Capt. David Duffie, USN, Requirements and Force Structure Division (J55), U.S. Pacific Command

Col. Mark Freitas, USMC, Chief, Plans and AOR Division (J35), Operations and Plans Directorate, U.S. Joint Forces Command

Ms. Lisa Gordon-Hagerty, Director for Weapons of Mass Destruction Preparedness, National Security Council

Captain Harlan Henderson, USCG, Commander, National Strike Force, U.S. Coast Guard National Strike Force Coordination Center, U.S. Coast Guard

Mr. Jack A. Kelly, Senior Research Associate, Institute for Foreign Policy Analysis (IFPA)

Mr. Paul Kurtz, Director for Critical Infrastructure, National Security Council

Mr. Richard Owens, Disaster Operations Specialist, Office of Foreign Disaster Assistance, U.S. Agency for International Development

Mr. H.K. Park, Office of the Assistant Chief of Staff to the Secretary of Defense and Assistant to the Secretary of Defense for Civil Support, Office of the Secretary of Defense

Dr. Charles M. Perry, Vice President and Director of Studies, Institute for Foreign Policy Analysis (IFPA)

Lt. Eric Runnels, USCG, Response Operations Division, U.S. Headquarters, U.S. Coast Guard

Mr. James L. Schoff, Program Officer, U.S.-Japan Foundation

BG Robert Summers, USAF, Director, Combat Support Directorate, Defense Threat Reduction Agency

RADM Donald Weiss, USN, Director of Asian and Pacific Affairs, International Security Affairs, Office of the Secretary of Defense

Ms. Lisa Weldon, Planning and Coordination Branch, Operations and Planning Division, Response and Recovery Directorate, Federal Emergency Management Agency

Agenda
Second IFPA-OSIPP Workshop

Enhancing U.S.-Japanese Cooperation on Crisis & Consequence Management
April 10-11, 2002, ANA Hotel, Tokyo, Japan

Wednesday, April 10

WELCOME AND INTRODUCTION

Professor Mitsuru Kurosawa, former Dean, OSIPP, Osaka University

Dr. Charles M. Perry, Vice President, IFPA

Mr. David Shear, Minister Counselor for Political Affairs, US Embassy, Japan

SESSION 1

Scope of the Crisis: Impact of a Large-scale Earthquake on Greater Tokyo, Japan, and U.S. Installations in and around Tokyo

Co-chaired by *Prof. Kurosawa* and *Dr. Perry*

This session provided the basis for follow-on discussions, laying out the potential damage that a major earthquake could have on the Tokyo area, including U.S. military and other installations

Presentations

On potential damage a large earthquake around Tokyo could cause (description and analysis of notional scenario)

Professor Toshiyuki Shikata, Teikyo University and Advisor to Governor of Tokyo

Japan's Crisis Management Legislative Initiatives

Mr. Shigenobu Tamura, Staff, Policy Research Board of Liberal Democratic Party, and Lecturer, Graduate School of Law, Keio University.

Disaster Impact: U.S. Military Facilities Japan

Lt. Col. Joseph Jacky, U.S. Forces Japan/J-52

Open Discussion

SESSION 2

Crisis/Consequence Management and Cooperation: Lessons and Current Mechanisms

Co-chaired by *Prof. Toshiyuki Shikata*, Teikyo University, and advisor to the governor of Tokyo, and *Dr. Perry*

This session outlined the crisis and consequence management coordination and cooperation mechanisms currently in place and the initial responses to the crisis that would be undertaken by the Japanese government at the various levels (national, local) and the U.S. government, both in Washington and at facilities in and around Tokyo. It also reviewed lessons learned on crisis and consequence management from Hanshin and September 11, to include priorities that arise in the event of a terrorist act.

Presentations

Conceptual Framework of Crisis and Consequence Management

Lt. Col. Juichi Araki, Air Staff Office, Japan Defense Agency

On current mechanisms on government crisis management and questions

Mr. Masanori Nishi, Director Public Affairs, Japan Defense Agency

Lessons of the 1995 Kobe Earthquake and Challenges of DRI

Dr. Shingo Nagamatsu, Research Scientist, Disaster Reduction and Human Renovation Institution (DRI)

U.S. and Bilateral Crisis Management Mechanisms in Japan
Lt. Col. Wendell Sims, USA, USFJ/J52

Disaster Relief and Crisis Management and How States and Localities Plan and Coordinate with National Level Agencies
Mr. Richard Swensen, Director of Commonwealth Security, Commonwealth of Massachusetts

Post September 11, 2001: Lessons Learned and Implications for Homeland Security, Crisis, and Consequence Management
Dr. Jacquelyn K. Davis, Executive Vice President, IFPA

Open Discussion

SESSION 3
Critical Infrastructure Dimensions of the Crisis
Co-chaired by **Prof. Satoshi Morimoto**, Takushoku University, and **Dr. Jacquelyn K. Davis**, executive vice president, IFPA

This session examined specifically the damage that an earthquake or similar catastrophic event would do to critical infrastructures, particularly telecommunications and cyber links, in Tokyo, and how such damage would severely complicate response and coordination of Japanese and U.S. efforts.

Presentations
Concept of Critical Infrastructure Assurance
Mr. Michael Vatis, Director of the Institute for Security Technology Studies at Dartmouth College
Critical Infrastructure Damage from September 11 Attacks
Dr. Andrew C. Winner, Senior Staff Member, IFPA

Open Discussion

Group Visit to Tokyo Metropolitan Disaster Prevention Center at Tokyo Metropolitan Government Office, Shinjuku, Tokyo

Thursday, April 11

SESSION 4

Cyber Attacks Complicating Response and Management
Co-chaired by **MG Noboru Yamaguchi, JGSDF**, and **Dr. Davis**

This session explored a contingency whereby an unknown entity conducts ongoing cyber attacks on Japanese and Japan-based U.S. cyber infrastructures in the aftermath of the earthquake, complicating coordination, communication, and response efforts. This variation adds complexity to response and brings in law enforcement, intelligence, and cyber response teams.

Presentations

GOJ Cyber Defense History and Cyber Response Mechanisms
Mr. Yasuhisa Ishizuka, Director, Accounting Division, General Affairs Department, Defense Facilities Administration Agency
Cyber Threat and Policy of Japan
Mr. Sugio Takahashi, Researcher, the National Institute of Defense Studies.
U.S. Cyber Response Mechanisms
Mr. Michael Vatis, Director of the Institute for Security Technology Studies at Dartmouth College

Open Discussion

SESSION 5

Hazardous Materials Releases, Unknown Toxins, and Response Options
Co-chaired by **Ambassador Ryukichi Imai** and **Dr. Perry**

This session discussed the release of hazardous or environmentally damaging materials or substances due to the earthquake, and the detection of the use of toxins/WMD of unknown origin and reviewed the capabilities and responses of Japanese government authorities and U.S. facilities and authorities in place and in the continental United States (CONUS) to respond to these incidents. Focus was on coordination of hazmat/accident response and containment/cleanup capabilities and the need to identify, deter, and/or apprehend any assailant making use of toxins to increase destruction and chaos.

Presentation

GOJ Response Capabilities

Mr. Tsutomu Arai, Planning Director, Center for Disarmament and Non-Proliferation Promotion, the Japan Institute of International Affairs

USCINCPAC Foreign Consequence Management (CM)

Lt. Col. Michael W. Callaghan, USMC, Chemical Plans and MSCA Planner, U.S. Pacific Command

U.S. Hazardous Materials and Cross Border Cleanup Capabilities

Capt. James Garrett, U.S. Coast Guard

Open Discussion

Participants
Second IFPA-OSIPP Workshop

JAPAN

Mr. Nobumasa Akiyama, Assistant Professor, Hiroshima Peace Institute, Hiroshima City University

Mr. Yukihiko Akutsu (The Democratic Party of Japan), Member of House of Representatives

Mr. Tsutomu Arai, Research Director, Center for Disarmament and Non-Proliferation Promotion, The Japan Institute of International Affairs (JIIA)

Lt. Col. Junichi Araki (Japan Air SDF), Plans and Programs Division, Air Staff Office, Japan Defense Agency

Col. Koichirou Bansho (Japan Ground SDF), Chief, Policy and Programs Section, Plans and Operations Department, Ground Staff Office, Japan Defense Agency

Lt. Col. Hiroshi Egawa, C41 System Securities Section, Maritime Staff Office, Japan Defense Agency

Professor Robert D. Eldridge, Associate Professor, Osaka School of International Public Policy (OSIPP), Osaka University

Maj. Gen. Fumio Eto (Japan Ground SDF), Director, Plans and Operations Department, Ground Staff Office, Japan Defense Agency

Lt. Col. Riichi Furugaki, Procurement Division, Air Staff Office, Japan Defense Agency

Mr. Hiroo Hieda, Director, Center for Technology and International Affairs (CTIA), The Institute for Future Technology

Dr. Toshiya Hoshino, Associate Professor, International Politics and Security, Osaka School of International Public Policy, Osaka University

Mr. Ryukichi Imai, Distinguished Research Fellow, Institute for International Policy Studies

Mr. Yasuhisa Ishizuka, Director, Accounting Division, General Affairs Department, Defense Facilities Administration Agency

Mr. Kuniharu Kakihara, Sr. Research Fellow, Institute for International Policy Studies

Mr. Seichi Kanise, Journalist

Maj. Nobuo Kano (Japan Ground SDF), Land Digitalization Group, Ground Staff Office, Japan Defense Agency

Dr. Takashi Kawakami, Professor, Hokuriku University

Dr. Mitsuru Kurosawa, former Dean, Osaka School of International Public Policy, Osaka University

Mr. Akira Mizutani, Counselor, National Security Affairs and Crisis Management, Cabinet Secretariat

Professor Satoshi Morimoto, Professor, Faculty of International Development, Takushoku University

Dr. Shingo Nagamatsu, Researcher, Disaster Reduction and Human Renovation Institution (DRI)

Col. Shigenori Nakano (Japan Ground SDF), Chief, Land Digitalization Group, Plans and Operations, Ground Staff Office, Japan Defense Agency

Mr. Masanori Nishi, Director of Public Affairs, Japan Defense Agency

Professor Hitoshi Okada, Associate Professor, National Institute of Informatics

LCDR Ryo Sakai, International Policy Plans and Programs Division, Maritime Staff Office, Japan Defense Agency

Professor Toshiyuki Shikata, Professor, The Teikyo University

Lt. Col. Kazuto Shimizu (Japan Ground SDF), 2nd Operations Section, Ground Office, Japan Defense Agency

Mr. Sugio Takahashi, Researcher, the National Institute for Defense Studies

Col. Miho Takemoto, Chief of C41 System Securities Section, Maritime Staff Office, Japan Defense Agency

Mr. Takeo Takuma, Vice President, Director, Tokyo Office, The United States – Japan Foundation

Mr. Shigenobu Tamura, Staff, Policy Research Board of Liberal Democratic Party, Lecturer, Graduate School of Law, Keio University

Mr. Koutarou Tanaka, Deputy Counselor, National Security Affairs and Crisis Management, Cabinet Secretariat

Mr. Yosei Umetsu, Deputy Director, Defense Intelligence Division, Bureau of Defense Policy, Japan Defense Agency

Col. Shigeyuki Urano, Vice Director of Research and Development Department, Ground Research and Development Command, Ground Staff Office, Japan Defense Agency

Mr. Yuji Wada, Future Navigator, Center for the 21st Century System, The Institute for Future Technology

Maj. Gen. Noboru Yamaguchi, Japan Ground SDF, Deputy Commandant, Aviation School, Camp Akeno

Col. Atsumasa Yamamoto, Director, Osaka Provincial Liaison Office

THE UNITED STATES

Lt. Kevin Bell, USN, US Forces Japan

Lt. Cdr. John Bellay, USN, US Forces Japan

Lt. Cdr. Le'Keen Brouwn USN, US Forces Japan

Lt. Col. Michael W. Callaghan, USMC, Chemical Plans and MSCA Planner, U.S. Pacific Command

Mr. Ralph A. Cossa, President, Pacific Forum, The Center for Strategic and International Studies (CSIS)

Dr. Jacquelyn K. Davis, Executive Vice President, Institute for Foreign Policy Analysis

Ms. Angela Eng, U.S. Embassy, Tokyo

Capt. James M. Garrett, Commander, Coast Guard Far East Activities

Mr. Blair Hall, Deputy Political Counselor, U.S. Embassy, Tokyo

Mr. Steven L. Herman, Flotilla Staff Officer – Communications Services, U.S. Coast Guard Auxiliary

Lt. Col. Joseph Jacky, USA, U.S. Forces Japan

Lt. Jill Lumpkin, USCG(r)

Dr. Charles M. Perry, Vice President and Director of Studies, Institute for Foreign Policy Analysis

Dr. James J. Przystup, Sr. Fellow and Research Professor, Institute of National Strategic Studies, National Defense University

Mr. David Shear, Political Counselor, U.S. Embassy, Tokyo

Mr. Kenji Shibachi, Protocol Officer and Liaison Officer, U.S. Coast Guard Activities Far East

Lt. Col. Wendell Sims, USA, U.S. Forces Japan

Col. Cosmas R. Spofford, USMC, Chief, Regional Strategy and Policy Division of the Strategic Planning and Policy Directorate, U.S. Pacific Command

Mr. Richard Swenson, Director of Commonwealth Security for Massachusetts

Mr. Peter VanBuren, U.S. Embassy, Tokyo

Mr. Michael Vatis, Institute for Security Technology Studies, Dartmouth College

Dr. Andrew Winner, Institute for Foreign Policy Analysis

CDR Edward Yeaste, USN, U.S. Forces Japan